Here's what reade

Being In ıvıy ɒoɑy

"Toni has gifted us with a readable and rich handbook on how to deal with trauma. She carefully weaves well-researched information with examples and healing techniques. Toni stays with you as you read and you can feel her compassion coming through."

David Richo, PhD: Author of *When the Past is Present* (Shambhala)

♥

"Being In My Body *is a testimony both to Toni Rahman's personal work and her professional and clinical skills.*
This book is not only easy to read and understand, but interesting and informative.

"*Toni does an excellent job of explaining the different kinds of trauma, which is an important contribution to the field of traumatology.*

"*I found myself feeling comfortable in my own body as I read her book, which told me that she was in HER body as she was writing it.*

"*Most of all, I appreciate Toni's open-hearted writing style, and her compassionate approach towards herself, her family, her clients and her readers.*"

Janae B. Weinhold, PhD LPC, Co-author of *Developmental Trauma: The Game Changer in the Mental Health Profession, Counterdependency: The Flight From Intimacy & Breaking Free of the Codependency Trap*

"Being In My Body *is a beautiful synthesis of powerful teachings, practices, and stories that have helped me tremendously in my still-unfolding journey towards greater self-understanding, self-acceptance, and embodiment. Toni Rahman has helped me understand the ways in which I experienced developmental trauma, how it has impacted me, and perhaps most importantly, what I can do about it in the present moment. This book has left me feeling empowered, supported, and deeply understood. I have read many books that touch on these topics and themes, and what I found most unique about this book was Toni's willingness to be vulnerable and open with her readers. As I read* Being In My Body, *I felt like I was being accompanied through difficult terrain by a gentle guide who was willing to share her own journey in the hopes that it would help others along on theirs. In my case, it certainly has, and I hope that many others will benefit as well."*

- Megan Farmer, Postgraduate Psychology Student, Calif.

♥

Being In My Body:

What You Might Not Have Known About Trauma, Dissociation & The Brain

By Toni Rahman, MSW, LCSW

Columbia, Missouri

Cover Design by Trina Brunk
Photos by Julio Tonatiu Reyes Chavez

Published, printed and distributed in the United States
by Open Sesame Publishing.

Columbia, Missouri

Acknowledgements

I would like to thank my sister, Tracy, for her protective love, care, and guidance throughout my life, for the ways she inspires me and opens doors of awareness and knowledge for me and so many others. Thank you, dear, for your steadfast love, wisdom and support. The ways you share your courageous heart on this planet leave it better and us richer. I can only imagine who I might be today had it not been for you, your caring and your generous heart.

For being the two biggest motivators for staying conscious and responsible in my adult relationships and showing me how it's done, I have my two daughters to thank. I adore your beautiful souls.

I would also like to thank the launch team for their extraordinary support, input and encouragement, with special thanks for editorial support from Stephanie Brooks, Suzanne Norton, and Tracy Barnett. Trina Brunk, I have a very special place in my heart for you, but I will cherish forever the memory of sitting at your kitchen table creating the design for this cover. You have been there with me every step of the way, and I thank heaven for you. Thank you Tami, Tanya, Aany, Tasha for the inspiration you always provide and for your love. You (my siblings) were the ones who first taught me about joy and pleasure in just the right measure; you were the standard against which all my subsequent experiences were measured, and still are. I love you so very much!

Kenny Greene, thank you for introducing me to the world of moving meditation, of tai chi and chi kung, and for your generosity in teaching and sharing what you know. It would be impossible to measure the impact you have made in the world in these terms alone. For my part, not a day goes by that I don't draw on your teachings about caring for the body, using it in an efficient way, about owning my power and the many, many wisdom nuggets you share in your free classes at the Armory. Thank you for making an appearance in this book. Your example of service and discipline are a gift to me and countless others.

And last, but certainly not least, I would like to thank my clients, especially the ones who so graciously allowed me to use their stories. You have all given me so much, and in so many ways that I am still trying to digest and understand. Thank you, from the bottom of my heart.

Dedication

Now more than ever before, I have the ability to feel gratitude for the times my mother so adeptly attuned to my needs, given all the challenges she faced. And there is no denying the enduring support, adoration, attention and warmth I received from my father. And in this felt sense of gratitude for them both, and the forgiveness I feel for all of us, I can physically sense myself opening to their love and an even greater love for life. As I continue to learn how to open myself to receiving life's sweetness, I see how not feeling safe had kept me tightly closed.

That attunement was completely and appropriately available to me is evident in my ability to feel bonded with my children and connect deeply with my siblings. And I am who I am today in very large part due to the care and dedication and resources that went into my upbringing. Though there are passages in this book that express my infant rage and my 14-year-old rancor and disdain, I have my parents to thank for so very much, not the least of which are my fabulous siblings. I cherish each and every one of them. And I embrace this task of working on, building up and healing any social or emotional deficits that originated due to the economic stressors and intergenerational trauma that characterized my childhood home.

Table of Contents

Chapter 5 - Healthy Adult Intimacy 150

Chapter 6 - The Body as a Bridge to The Self..................177

Foreword

It has been my great honor and privilege to learn and grow as a martial artist, and to share what I know with others. Along the way I have worked with many warriors and survivors of trauma who find tai chi, also known as tae ji, to be useful for managing pain, stress and the wounds they bear from their literal and figurative "battlefields" of life. Tai chi offers tremendous benefits as a means of self-defense, physical exercise and meditation as well as a means for community building and social support.

Meditation is universally recognized as a tool for stress reduction and personal development. Tai chi, as a form of moving meditation, is accessible to many people who cannot tolerate sitting meditation, as it keeps the mind occupied, and gives the practitioner a set of very specific goals to strive for but it does not restrict the practitioner to static or difficult postures. As such, it provides an excellent practice for people at any stage of life and any level of physical development who wish to optimize the use of their bodies and physical capabilities. There are a great number of styles and approaches; standing, seated or prone. Some recommend music, focus objects, candles, incense and isolation. Each practitioner will find what is most effective for them.

Many teachers divide a tai chi regimen into five content areas. These are solo meditation, a set of warm-up exercises, form work, form correction and applications and the practice of push hands.

Warm-up exercises are abundant. One can choose a variety that will activate the major muscle groups and move top to bottom for grounding. Working from bottom to top increases energy.

Form work advances from simple to complex performances. The continuous, smooth, evenly linked postures are designed to become a moving meditation that builds on the benefits of static practices. Through dedicated practice, a practitioner can gain muscle strength, health, coordination, and a greater mastery of his or her body.

Form corrections and applications are meant to develop strategies for making the forms more precise. Form helps a practitioner deepen the understanding of the tai chi principles, i.e., breathing, posture and unified movement of the body. Form theory can be supported and informed by study of the five energy phases, qi gong and other aspects of traditional Chinese medicine. The application of individual moves of postures makes clearer the Chinese origins of tai chi. Learning is enhanced and deepened when Chinese teachers join the group and share their knowledge, or simply when friends and fellow players share their understandings of this great martial art.

Push hands is a practice that calls upon the practitioner to engage with an opponent in an experiential field where the pair can practice meeting the force and flow of one another's energy, moving with and exploring their combined energy, anticipating areas of weakness and strength, and maintaining balance when in close proximity to the other.

The book you hold in your hands incorporates and distills much energy, research, and work. It is a product of much thought and experience, and is a well-organized synthesis of Toni's personal progress and journey to overcome complex trauma. It will serve for many as a template for gaining a better understanding about trauma and dissociation. The synthesis and amassing of resources and instructional material is exemplary. But in presenting this book we also have first hand, tangible proof of its author's caring and compassion. She and I travel a similar path in striving for mastery and balance through empathy, service and action, which are potent antidotes for those who have searched for health and understanding and not found them in more mainstream or logical places.

– Master Kenneth L. Greene

Overview

As a trauma specialist, I have been offered glimpses into other people's lives as they make steps, tentative and bold, steady and halting, toward reclaiming their lives from the devastation of trauma. They have touched and inspired me so deeply, and I am so grateful to them all. In a way, my clients have healed me and grown me up. And in this light, I can include myself among these pages in hopes of helping you see how all of this relates to you, too, whether you identify with the idea of not being fully in your body, you have had trouble maintaining deep and nourishing connections in your closest relationships, or you have a friend or loved one who has been touched by some kind of trauma.

What I've noticed is that the very word "trauma" has a exclusionary effect, since so many automatically exempt themselves, saying that nothing "that bad" had ever happened to them.

At issue here is a topic that has only recently been connected with trauma at all, and is still largely circumvented by the establishment. It has to do with something my mentors are now referring to as developmental trauma or early relational trauma.[1] Whatever we call it, it has profound effects on our physical, interpersonal and mental health. It disconnects us from others, hinders development of a healthy sense of self, and makes safety in intimate relationships virtually unachievable until it is properly dealt with. I will discuss trauma in Chapter 1.

Trauma, whether it originates from an accident, the battlefield, or not having our developmental needs met during the first years of life, leaves its unique signature on our systems. In so many ways it disconnects us from ourselves and ourselves from the love and support of the world around us. I am going to call this disconnect, in its very broadest sense, dissociation. And I'm going to go so far as to say that virtually none of us gets through this life unscathed. That's why I'd like to pluck this mysterious and deeply complex subject—trauma and dissociation—out of the research realms and plop it into your lap, so you can see and know how it affects *all* of us. Once we have a better understanding of what it actually is, we can much more easily recognize it when we see it, which is vitally important. Only then can we care for ourselves and others appropriately and take the steps needed to prevent and overcome it.

Much of what I am about to tell you is inspired by my past, since from this relatively grown-up place, I can look back and see what recovery looks and feels like. In hindsight, I see a curious and somewhat disturbing pattern that I've come to term "intimacy disorder." How else does one explain

2

attracting one depressed, emotionally unavailable and/or addicted partner after another? Or answer for the destruction and expenditure of energy, time, and life force that accompany three separations and divorces? Not to mention the impact of all this on the children. Were these partners truly depressed, emotionally unavailable and/or addicted? Or was it something I did; something in the patterns of my relating with them that fostered or encouraged those characteristics? Was it just me projecting my own depression, emotional unavailability, and/or addictive tendencies?

Put in more concrete terms, I can now see that something obviously went wrong with me in the intimacy department. The most obvious indications were 1) intimacy had not been enduring, 2) intimacy had not been restorative, and 3) intimacy had not felt safe. In assessing this understanding, and doing what I can to correct it, I collect information, I sort, I digest.

Maybe a good place to start talking about all this is with an idea called regression. John Lee, in his book, *Growing Yourself Back Up*, has a lot to say about regression. As I scan my past intimate relationships, I see now how often and how unknowingly I would regress. Regression, says Lee, is what happens to us when, emotionally, we leave the present moment.

> *By contrast, staying present with yourself, your partner, your children, friends, colleagues, and boss means that, emotionally, you are completely in the here and now, and that a small part of you is neither wandering over the hills and valleys of your past nor trying to predict the future. While staying present is one*

of the greatest gifts you can give to yourself and others, it is much easier said than done.

When we regress, we go from being clear-thinking adults to talking, acting, and sometimes even looking like children who are not getting their way. We feel powerless and out of control, as if we don't have choices. We think we know what others need, but at the moment, we can't say what we ourselves need.[2]

Naming it, of course, helps. This thing happens, and I, for one, don't like it one bit. It wreaks havoc with my closest relationships, batters and confuses my children, obliterates my dignity, my sense of having some agency, some control over my life. Why do we do this?

I have come to recognize the symptoms of this thing called *Intimacy Disorder* in my patterns of relating. That much I know. Much of the thinking I do is trying to figure out what I should attribute this disorder to. As one sister said one Thanksgiving in an attempt to empathize, "something *happened* to you, didn't it?" I had to laugh (probably too hard, and for too long). No doubt, things had happened to her, too. But she had managed to stay in a loving relationship with her partner since their marriage thirty-two years and eight children ago. She is four years younger than me. Her way of acting out as a teen included butting heads with our parents, demanding her personal rights, and talking to her boyfriend all hours of the night on the telephone in hushed, serious tones (all the things that a healthy, developmentally appropriate teenager is supposed to do). Me—well, acting out was something I did while simultaneously maintaining the image of a "good girl." This included sneaking around, lying well, and counting the days until I could leave that place and begin making a home of my own. For me, the only solution I could imagine was through physical escape.

Seven Generations

An ecological concept said to originate from the Iroquois Nation states is: *In every deliberation, we must consider the impact on the seventh generation.* While listening to Peter Levine in 2014,[3] in an interview series on trauma, I heard of this seven-generation theme, again credited to Native American thought. Levine told of spending time with the Navajo healers in Arizona, where he learned that the Navajo had particular rituals that they did when their soldiers returned from war with other Indian tribes. They realized, he said, that if the soldier came back and brought the trauma into the community, it would affect the entire tribe for seven generations.

It is clear that the soldier has been traumatized. And the ways that it affects him are obvious to his family and community from his actions, his reactivity, his ways of coping. But what does it look like, say, three generations down? What about that seventh generation? Is it so small, by that time, as to even be relevant? I am fascinated by the healing work that happens under my care, and I also do quite a bit of thinking about the people I see outside of the clinical setting. People who tell me their stories, and people I have chosen as intimate partners in the past. I think a lot about how those relationships mark the trajectory of my own growth and development—signposts, if you will—that in retrospect offer much to ponder indeed.

Stress and the Brain

Something happens in the brain as a result of stress. And prolonged stress in early life, over time, tends to result in the potential for *overload*, which stands in the way of our access to the parts of the brain that are in charge of discerning between the *here and now* and the *there and then*. It's not a matter of discipline or manners or learning, and is completely unaffected by determination, or the power of will. Such overload catapults us out of the "now" and drops us into a feeling state of a particular unresolved "then." The same executive command cuts us off from the parts of our brain where we have stored adaptive things we have learned since childhood, and the ability to engage in logical thought and narrative speech.

This pattern is all too common in people who have been traumatized. But it is a function of the brain that can happen within all of us to one degree or another. As strange as it sounds, we can attribute our survival as a species to this function, because it actually helps ensure survival.

For those of us with memories that constitute unresolved trauma, the brain can react in a very specific way. When it detects something that resembles a past, yet-to-be reconciled set of circumstances, we might find ourselves disconnected from our ability to take in new information from the present, and we are flooded with the emotions and body sensations that were recorded and stored from the earlier event. These are what we refer to as unprocessed memories. And to make matters even worse, this disconnect which happens at an automatic, unconscious level, sends us into a mindless impulse or action; at a physical level, we respond in the way we responded in the past. For me, it's the visceral response of feeling unsafe and trapped, and needing to escape when in intimate relationship with another. My body shields itself by tensing up, and I project my awareness outside of myself, scanning the physical and emotional environment, constantly assessing the status and emotional state of the other. Again, it's not a matter of choosing this response. It happens beneath the level of consciousness. We will talk more about this in Chapter 1, where we go into more depth about trauma.

Another piece of the puzzle that comes together to help me know I don't have to stay an out-of-control child forever is the idea of an emotional flashback. Thanks to author and therapist Pete Walker, in his book *Complex PTSD: From Surviving to Thriving: A Guide and Map for Recovering from Childhood Trauma,*[4] I now have a concept that helps me understand the storm inside me that I can now identify as an emotional flashback. What I see in my mind's eye is the image of a child kicking and screaming, completely out of control. What the child needs is help learning to regulate her emotions—something children do not have the capability to do without the help of adults. She does not need to be shamed or punished for losing control. The image helps me have compassion for myself. In essence, I can now be the adult, calmly holding space for the child while the adrenaline surges, subtly moving myself into a position where I might do minimal damage, and when I have had a chance to somewhat return to my senses, to help myself understand and learn from what has happened and make any necessary amends or repairs. I also know that what is happening to "her" is that she is essentially reliving a feeling state, that her logical brain has been hijacked, and that the past is flooding back, obscuring anything that she has learned about being powerful, resourced or safe. And since I now understand what a flashback is, I know that there will be an end to it, and that I will be able to work with what I have just experienced and to know more about myself, my needs and my wounding, and in knowing this, I can heal. We will talk more about flashbacks in Chapter 2.

It is probably a good time to acknowledge Barry and Janae Weinhold and the legions of researchers and thinkers in the field of attachment and early relational trauma. Thanks to these folks we can understand more and more about what developmental needs are, and how not having our developmental needs met can have the same or even a more profound effect than physical abuse on the development of our brains and psyches, setting the stage for dissociation and more trauma. Dan Siegel goes so far as to say that when we look at the impact of both neglect and abuse in childhood, neglect was just as, if not more negatively impactful, as overt abuse.[5] We will go into attachment and parenting in more depth in Chapter 3.

Still other pieces of the puzzle drop into place for me as I consider longer-standing feelings of not being friends with my body, not feeling like I have experienced fully the sense of embodiment I want, and knowing, at deeper and deeper levels, what that might be like. The work of Pat Ogden, Stephen Porges, John Sarno, Peter Levine and so many, many others is coming together into a cathartic whole, helping me understand that the body is an incredible, finely calibrated instrument, and that many of us require some instruction before we can properly use it to help us navigate our lives. In his book, *In An Unspoken Voice*, Peter Levine says,

> *Traumatized people are fragmented and disembodied. The constriction of feeling obliterates shade and texture, turning*

everything into good or bad, black or white, for us or against us. It is the unspoken hell of traumatization. In order to know who and where we are in space and to feel that we are vital, alive beings, subtleties are essential. Furthermore, it is not just acutely traumatized individuals who are disembodied; most Westerners share a less dramatic but still impairing disconnection from their inner sensate compasses.[6]

Imagine the quality of life we would experience as Westerners if our whole culture experienced a shift where each of us, all at once, was committed to embracing and considering these wondrous instruments that we possess, and using their wisdom along with our intellects in our day-to-day, moment-to-moment interactions with ourselves and others. This is my new idea of healthy intimacy. It is a life in which our response to an ache or a pain would not be to reach for a pill to make it go away or to distract ourselves to avoid feeling it. It would be a slowing down to listen, to tend, to be. It is a partnership with oneself, where one does not seek dominance over another, but seeks to dance in harmony, always placing the priority of returning to oneness and unity over any other possible goal.

Here is another idea: Could it be that the way in which we interface with our bodies is directly mirrored in the quality of the interactions we have with others and the world?

Pain
When I reached my mid-40's I began to notice that my body was in pain most of the time. I would notice and then try to ignore the pain, which was mostly in my back and neck. I decided that this was a function of age, and debated

whether, if it continued to worsen, I was interested in experiencing long life. (Recall that I had learned very early that escape, or shutting down emotionally and waiting for an opportunity to escape, was the only solution.) Luckily for me, the constant pain was one of the things that ultimately motivated me to develop a practice of *tai chi*, where I began to learn how to use movement and the wisdom of an ancient martial art to grow my awareness of my body and the value of living in the present moment. Incidentally, *tai chi* and gentle stretching are the only ways I have found to effectively manage my pain. When my practice drops off, my body reminds me, as the pain reliably returns.

One of those ideas with which I have more recently come into contact is the basic physiological knowledge that is coming out of so much of the research of the past fifteen or twenty years around The Polyvagal Theory,[7] and what it comes down to this: The mind and the body are indistinguishable from one another; the mind is not limited to the brain.

I suspect that my pain is—as pain in the large trunk muscles often tends to be—a result of repressed emotions. More specifically, the perception of pain in these muscles has been shown to be a result of stress-induced constriction, producing mild oxygen deprivation in particular muscles, that tells a story about how the body habitually deals with stress. How many of us have developed the habit of holding stress in the body as a way to avoid the uncomfortable feeling of emotions instead of feeling the emotions and allowing them to serve their intended functions as they occur? And if this has been our pattern for as long as we can remember, how would we know that this is not normal? John Sarno, MD, goes so far as to say that for some, there are "layers of unconscious rage being held in the muscles of your back."

> *It would appear that most cases of chronic back pain are actually caused not by spinal problems, but by muscle tension and spasm. This is not to be dismissed: it is extremely painful. Such muscle tension is caused by emotional tension, and the deeper that emotional tension is explored the more the story behind the pain is revealed. It may be a story of anger, fear, exhaustion, of trying to prove something to someone, of denial, of lack of forgiveness— whatever it is, it is in the back because it is well hidden there. But it also hurts.[8]*

If we were to take the time necessary to learn how we are actually using our bodies, we might have a little more compassion for ourselves and take steps toward using pain for its intended purpose: to inform us of problems as they arise, and to let us know when negotiation and change are called for. For those of us who learned to ignore our pain very early on, there is as much to unlearn as there is to learn.

Facilitating Boundaries 101,[9] beginning in 2011, my students and the circle we created together became my teacher. My understanding about the prerequisites for lasting intimacy in relationship began to deepen, along with my awareness of what was necessary to develop alliances that were trusting and safe. And it became more and more obvious to me how indispensable interpersonal boundaries and a certain level of skill in communicating about these boundaries were.

By this time I was able to coach my clients to scan their bodies for information, to guide them into the darkest recesses of their fears and their grief, leading them out, triumphant, with their personal power and their prizes by the end of each sweaty, tissue-soaked hour. Watching them, I learned what was possible, and gained the charts and maps necessary to plumb my own depths. I was slow to feel as they felt though, staying safely in the theoretical realm, not yet knowing quite how to apply it to myself. What I may be learning now is that not only do I need tools and boundaries to be safe and function in healthy ways with others, but that I also need tools to help me find my way back into my body. Elaine Aron talks about how we can learn to interface with our bodies in *The Highly Sensitive Person: How to Thrive When the World Overwhelms You*. She refers to something called the body-self.

> *Think of what the infant and the body have in common. First, both are wonderfully content and cooperative when they are not overstimulated, worn out, and hungry. Second, when babies and sensitive bodies really are exhausted, both are largely helpless to correct things on their own. The baby-you relied on a caretaker to set limits and satisfy your simple, basic needs, and your body relies on you to do it now. Both also cannot use words to explain their troubles; they can only give louder and louder signals for help or develop a symptom so serious it cannot be ignored. The wise caretaker knows that much woe is avoided by responding to the infant/body at the first sign of distress. Finally [...] caretakers who think newborn babies or bodies can be spoiled and should be "left to cry" are wrong. Research*

demonstrates that if a small infant's crying is responded to promptly (except at those times when responding just adds to the overstimulation), that infant will cry less, not more, when older.[10]

I have wrapped myself in theories about what an asset it is to be able to use the body and information from our bodies to tell us that we have an unmet need asking us for our care and attention, and I have learned that one only needed to be *willing* to learn from this information to begin the road to recovery. And I heard myself telling my clients that they could strike a healthy balance between listening to the body, and becoming a slave to it, or letting it dictate the terms of their lives.

Cherishing and respecting my body and connecting with it so that I can better know who I am is something I did not learn from my parents. Nor, in so many cases, did our parents learn it from theirs. And I suspect that we are not alone in this. Intergenerational trauma is woven into the fabric of our modern world, with its effects coloring the lives of the descendants of African slaves, the children and other relatives of holocaust survivors and the descendants of native peoples from all over the globe. Those who survive great catastrophes like famine, genocide, war, and economic depression often suffer silently, and pass their unacknowledged pain on to their children. All of these groups live with the legacy of their ancestors' trauma, coping with the ins and outs of life the best they can, with a subtle knowing that something is not right, yet they are unable to name it. Well, something *is* wrong. And if it is not appropriately tended to, it passes from one generation to another, robbing individuals of their potential for joy, connection and contentment. In very big ways, it contributes to the disconnectedness we feel in our current culture, where, according to the Mayo Clinic in 2013, seventy percent of the US population is on at least one kind of pharmaceutical medication, and fifty percent is on more than two medications.[11] Kelly Brogan, MD, says that one in four women of reproductive age take medication for depression.[12] Most would admit being addicted to something, whether it's a drug, Facebook, a food/beverage, or work. And we have not a minute left over in our busy lives in which to even contemplate *what* we are distracting ourselves from.

Grace led me out of that place, and into a new one when I ended my private practice in Missouri and headed south. For me, I had to be physically removed from the rush and the needs of others, at least for a time, in order to feel me and learn to listen. To be with myself. To feel into my own process. And ever so tentatively, the bud of an idea presented itself to me from deep within the literature: *We are designed, from birth, to take refuge in the trusting bonds we have with others.* Something, however, had gone quite differently for me. Intimacy—the feeling that came with partnering—was a trigger that made my body react in a primitive "freeze" or "flight" kind of way.

When we are functioning properly in relationship, we have a whole range of responses to choose from, and we can follow both our instincts and logic to act in the most appropriate manner, using information that is available to us through our senses. When we are mature adults, we should be able to choose our responses, rather than being limited to or trapped in fixed or automatic responses.

People who are trapped in a trauma cycle, however, do not have this fluidity to think and respond in times of stress, particularly when the stress has to do with close relationships. Walker[13] identifies four types of responses, fight, flight, freeze, and fawn—the four f's—as being the patterns people with Complex Post Traumatic Stress Disorder (CPTSD) most often fall into. "With all 4F types," according to Walker, "the closeness of intimacy often triggers us into emotional flashbacks. Our 4F defenses therefore offer protection against further re-abandonment by precluding the type of vulnerable relating that leads to deeper bonding." We adopt one of these reactions, which then becomes frozen in place, and it limits us to a particular style of relating—all in the name of "protecting us" from the pain of intimacy.

I began to understand by looking back over one failed attempt to bond after another, that for me, intimacy was another word for annihilation; that it carried an unconscious directive to flee, with the ultimate effect of the unwitting abandonment of my self in the process. Approached from this unexplored emotional place, my relationships were anything but safe. And they were destined for failure before they even began.

Emotions

One thing that my clients have taught me is that a general understanding of emotions is indispensable in the process of integrating and recovering from trauma. This information is relevant particularly with regard to scary or unpleasant emotions. But it can also apply for many of us with regard to pleasurable ones as well. Bottom line: emotions are an essential part of living and sharing ourselves with others. None of our emotions are negative. They all offer us crucial information about ourselves and our needs.

The next couple of pages will be a basic but by no means comprehensive overview of emotions. I encourage you to look deeper into this topic. Karla McLaren[14] is one of my favorite thinkers about emotions, and she shares generously about her ideas online and in books which are great resources.

Let's start with the anatomy of an emotion. From a theoretical perspective, if a person is willing and able to engage an emotion, without avoiding it for one reason or another, it will pass in 90 seconds or less. In session, a lot of people tell me they experience an emotion like a wave. It starts out small and grows and swells. At the point that it feels so big as to become almost unbearable, it starts tapering off again until it has completely subsided. And all this happens in under two minutes. Of course, not all emotions will reach this level of intensity, but all of them are asking for our attention. There is healing in simply noticing them, and allowing them to pass.

Second of all, it's very common to suppress and avoid feelings because of trauma, abuse, or neglect in childhood. We will talk more about this in Chapter 4. Now before you jump to the defense of your parents, I want you to stop and open your mind. Of course our parents did the best they could, but it would not have been humanly possible to protect us from everything. And that doesn't make them bad parents, it's just how things go. And those difficult things that happened to us early in our lives have helped to shape us, and make us into the people we are today.

Some of us had horrible parents, and I'm pretty sure they did the best they could, too. But the reason we avoid negative feelings is that sometime during our childhood we experienced a moment so intense and we lacked the words to talk about it (or the support of a healthy, attuned adult), that it *was literally* unsafe to feel the intensity of that emotion. In our childhood minds, feeling that feeling would have meant the end of us, so we put the feeling away, and moved on the best we could. I like to think of the intense energy of that childhood emotion as a cyst—walled off from awareness, but most certainly still there. And in many ways still affecting our lives. The energy of a typical cyst will begin to leak out in moments when we push ourselves past our own healthy limits, or when we are tired or hungry. In times like these we will naturally be more likely to fall into patterns we were talking about earlier with John Lee's idea about regression.

Fast forward ten or twenty or thirty years to today. As adults, we've had some time to gain resources. Certainly all our lives have changed since we were children. Through our experiences, we've acquired wisdom and maturity, and we have become physically larger. As adults, we're no longer dependent on other people to meet all our needs. Now if we need something, we can go to the store and get it. We have more vocabulary to talk about what upsets us. Still, we are riddled with cysts that exist below our consciousness, and there's a part of us that still believes that we'll self-destruct if we ever go near those emotions again.

And while it may have been true that our younger selves could not have tolerated these intense emotions, the truth of the matter is, feeling the emotions is the only way to eliminate the cysts once and for all. And now it is possible. Whether you learn to do it safely on your own, or you need, for a time, the help and support of a good therapist and/or bodyworker, you will be well rewarded for your efforts.

Unfortunately, as we age, it becomes more and more difficult to suppress and ignore these emotional cysts. It actually seems to require substantial energy just to keep them unconscious. Furthermore, carrying them around with us, unexamined, makes us more vulnerable to manipulation, and makes us easy targets for abuse. They also represent blind spots—places where we can unknowingly slide into versions of our less-resourced younger selves. As long as this information remains unprocessed, all our attempts at boundary setting are just going to lack the steam and energy of powerful adult boundaries and limits.

Tending to cysts is not something you want or need to take on all at once. And it's not something you want to do unsupported. As we move into the content of this material, you may experience strong emotions. This is good. I want you to know that you will not self-destruct, and that with a little coaching, you will be able to move through each emotion to its completion. The more you learn to put neutral attention on your emotions as they come up, the more of your past you will put behind you.

So while you move through this material, notice your emotions, because they can be important cues, helping you reconstruct the story you need to tell to move forward. Briefly notice where you feel the emotion in your body. For just a few seconds, put your attention into noticing, like a scientist might notice, how this sensation feels—as if you were feeling it for the very first time.

If you find yourself becoming distracted by emotions every couple of minutes, and you're attending to emotions to the extent that you are unable to be present for other things, begin to keep a small note pad to write them down, and then come back to them later. For this purpose, some people use specially created containers as temporary storage devices for their emotions that need more attention than they can give just now. Imagine, for instance, that you have a large Tupperware canister where you can safely put this emotion until you can attend to it. That is, when you have adequate time and support to be really present with it. This is not the same as stuffing or ignoring our emotions. The difference is that we will no longer just ignore our feelings. We now know they need tending to, and that we can safely do this tending over time. Do remember though, they are a lot like children. If you forget them, or neglect them, they will find a way to get your attention. And the more you ignore them, the more unruly they will become.

Here are just a few basic exercises you can practice to stay connected with your body while calming your nervous system. You can use them if you notice yourself beginning to feel overwhelmed in any situation. Many trauma survivors have found that they help them feel more grounded, less reactive, and more equipped to handle emotions as they arise. Sometimes just having such resources can help you avoid experiencing the emotions as threatening, but rather as useful information. They can also help you come back to the present if you suspect that your nervous system is overwhelmed, and you are in some kind of flashback.

Earth, Water, Wind and Fire
Earth — Notice the weight of your body, and what is supporting it. If you are sitting, notice where your body comes in contact with your chair, and any other sensations available to you with regard to this support. Notice your feet on the floor. Notice the details of the things around you.

Water — Make saliva. When we are in crisis, our digestive system is put on hold, and we stop producing saliva. Consciously notice any wetness in your mouth, take a tiny sip of water or think about something juicy and delicious. This can help you to produce saliva and send the message to your brain that you are actually okay.

Wind — Notice your breath. Notice the rise and fall of your chest or your belly, and the sensation of the air as it enters and leaves your nostrils and moves in and out of your lungs and air passages.

Fire — Fire up your imagination. Imagine a place where you feel permission to be exactly who you are right now. It may be a place in nature, or it might just be your room. You can make it exactly the way you want it to be. Imagine being there right now, and notice how that is. Notice any colors or textures in this place that belongs only to you. Notice light patterns, temperature, or sounds that might tell you what time of day, and what season it is. Notice if there is any energy around you that you would like to acknowledge, any animals, people or spirits. Notice any smells, and notice where your body is, in relation to the earth. Are you sitting or walking or lying down? What is supporting your body? What feelings do you notice? Next, decide where you would like to store this feeling in your body, so you can find it again when you need it. Take a moment to enjoy this place you have created in your imagination.

Feeling as Conscious Attention

I have yet to meet a trauma survivor who tells me they've never experienced confusion, or were unfamiliar with a sensation of guardedness or restriction. Trauma survivors are generally comfortable enough noticing and talking about *less constriction*, or *more relaxation*, *lightness*, or *spaciousness*. As we work through their traumas, I often watch, with wonder, the evidence of softening, from the outside. Apparently confusion, guardedness, and restriction are feelings that even the most emotion-averse person can identify and name. And that is good enough. Little by little, the more vulnerable emotions (shame, sadness, fear, terror) and the ones that had before been forbidden (anger, disdain, resentment) are allowed into awareness, felt and released.

By the time we reach adulthood, we've received so much misinformation about emotions, that unless we dedicate a significant amount of time and energy to untangling it, our emotions remain a dark unexplored realm inside of us far too dangerous to enter. Unfortunately, ignoring it does not make it go away.

In my clinical practice, I rely heavily on physical symptoms that clients tell me about in the history-taking phase of our work together, and along the course of treatment. During the processing of trauma, especially through the use of Eye Movement Desensitization and Reprocessing (EMDR), there is often increased bodily awareness, including the re-emergence of feelings and sensations originally experienced at the time of the trauma, and emotions experienced in the present that come through in waves, sometimes leaving the client with an initiation of sorts into the world of adult emotion; always offering a new way of seeing their traumatic experience, and connecting them with their own strength.

For those who feel like they missed the boat when it came to emotional tutelage, what we work together to develop is a practice of asking ourselves what we *might* be feeling emotionally, when we notice something (in the form of a visceral sensation, a pain or a tense muscle) asking us for our attention. We might ask, *What might I be feeling anxious (or angry or disappointed or embarrassed or vulnerable) about?* Asking these questions can sometimes help us connect with the emotion that we had been suppressing. Walker gives an excellent description of how feelings and emotions work.

> *Feeling 'occurs' when we direct our attention to an emotionally or physically painful state, and surrender to this experience without resistance. When we relax acceptingly into our pain, we can learn to gently absorb it into our experience. Feeling then functions as if our awareness is a solvent that dissolves and metabolizes the affect, energy and sensation of our emotions.*[15]

Awareness is powerful medicine. In other words, finding ways to bring consciousness to repressed emotions, and thus understanding, having compassion for, and ultimately releasing them is what John Sarno, MD, talks about when he refers to successful treatment of Tension Myositis Syndrome (TMS), which we will talk about more in Chapter 4.

Many people ask me what the difference is between feeling and emoting. Walker helps frame the distinction in the passage below.

> *Feeling is a subtler, [more] passive process than emoting. [...] Emoting is when we cry, anger*

out, or verbally ventilate the energy of an inner emotional experience. Feeling, on the other hand, is the inactive process of staying present to internal emotional experience without reacting. In recovery then, feeling is surrendering to our internal experiences of pain without judging or resisting them, and without emoting them out.[16]

The idea that emotional debris can accumulate in the body as a result of neglect, abuse, and other psychological trauma is one that I picked up along the way from various teachers, including John Upledger, Peter Levine, Pat Ogden, Stephen Porges, Mantak Chia and John Sarno, among many others. Recent research is also showing us that emotional debris can be passed from one generation to another through a phenomenon known as epigenetics. So now there is a rather broad collection of psychosomatic literature, research and anecdotal evidence to support what many mental health practitioners like me have learned by working with clients with unresolved trauma.

Physical pain is often nothing more than data being offered up by the subconscious mind, in attempts to make information (that is necessary for one to heal from trauma) available in a way that can be tolerated by the system; in a way that does not overwhelm, but refuses, nonetheless, to be ignored. Incidentally, this way may be so primitive or unfamiliar, that the person experiencing it is not likely to understand it without the help of an interpreter of sorts—a body-mind therapist, or someone who has experience in the language of the body. At any rate, the messages of the body are often what motivates a person to ask for and receive the help he or she needs to heal from an old emotional wound, and thus address the physical pain that alerted him or her to the fact that it was festering beneath the surface.

As therapists working in this way, we can address the pain as it presents itself, gently and with curiosity and compassion. In fact, it is very common to move, reduce, and eliminate such sensations in the course of one or two clinical sessions with mind-body therapies such as EMDR.

During my own journeys on the road to health and fuller consciousness, I have had a number of care professionals tell me that I held my body as though I were protecting myself from physical danger. In my 20's, one of my therapists described it as a physical armor, like a turtle shell, which I wore on my back and shoulders. He was curious about what might have happened to cause me to have such an armor. The next was a holistic chiropractor, half a decade later, who expressed his concern about whether I was getting the full nutritional value of my food, given what he described as my adrenaline system functioning in chronic overdrive, a condition that would compromise my immune and digestive systems, and eventually wear my body down, unless I could get a handle on it. More recently it was Barbara Rotthaler, a German naturopath, practicing in Mexico, who commented once more on the muscular "shell" I had produced through the chronic tension I habitually carry in my upper back and shoulders. I went to her for treatment because of a spasm I had in my right shoulder that left me incapacitated, with excruciating pain for the better part of two weeks. Finally, in a Resonance Repatterning session with an intuitive Mexican friend, Margarita, I was told that I "carried vulnerability in my body but I didn't feel it; I wasn't aware of it; that I was enclosed in a protected position in life, even when there was no danger." All of these things I knew at some level, though I had no idea how to fix them.

Another piece of the what-had-happened-to-me puzzle was just about to fall into place. These symptoms were leading me to the answer.

With each chapter of this book, I will share a story of an individual and their experience of embodiment and dissociation. Though each story is complex and may involve various types of dissociation, it lends itself as an example of a particular type, which I provide in the table below. Each has graciously given permission for me to share his or her story, but for their privacy I have changed their names.

Chapter	Individual Example	Type of Dissociation
Chapter 1: Trauma	Tracy	Fragmentation of Self
Chapter 2: Dissociation	Mel	Depersonalization
Chapter 3: Parenting	Toni	Emotional Flashback
Chapter 4: Body	Lu	Structural Separation
Chapter 5: Adult Intimacy	Robert	Structural Separation
Chapter 6: Bridge to Self	Nasreen	Fragmentation of Self

Chapter 1 - Trauma

In this discussion of embodiment and dissociation, the important idea of "trauma" is addressed in this chapter. When trying to understand trauma, it is important to know that there is a difference between *event trauma*, which refers to a specific traumatic event, and *complex trauma*, which occurs in infancy and childhood. Bessel van der Kolk, a Boston-based Dutch psychiatrist noted for his research in the area of post-traumatic stress since the 1970s, says that complex trauma

> *describes the experience of multiple and/or chronic and prolonged, developmentally adverse traumatic events, most often of an interpersonal nature (e.g., sexual or physical abuse, war, community violence) and early-life onset. These exposures often occur within the child's caregiving system and include physical, emotional, and educational neglect and child maltreatment beginning in early childhood.*[17]

It is well established that *event trauma* results in Post Traumatic Stress Disorder (PTSD), which we will talk about more below. *Complex trauma*, according to van der Kolk, has much broader significance in that it has pervasive effects on the development of the mind and brain and implications in all areas of health and functioning of the individual. Van der Kolk and his colleagues on The Complex Trauma Taskforce of the National Child Traumatic Stress Network[18] are therefore advocating for changes in the way children with behavioral problems are diagnosed. For children who have been difficult to diagnose because of acute and complicated symptoms, they are proposing a diagnosis of Developmental Trauma Disorder (DTD). According to van der Kolk, some of the symptoms that would be included in the DTD diagnosis would be:[19]

- complex disruptions of affect regulation
- disturbed attachment patterns
- rapid behavioral regressions and shifts in emotional states
- aggressive behavior against self and others
- failure to achieve developmental competencies
- loss of bodily regulation in the areas of sleep, food and self-care
- anticipatory behavior and traumatic expectations
- multiple somatic problems, from gastrointestinal distress to headaches
- self-hatred and self-blame
- chronic feelings of ineffectiveness

In the following chapters, the term *relational trauma* or *developmental trauma* will be used interchangeably with *complex trauma*.

Post Traumatic Stress Disorder (PTSD)

PTSD, as it is officially defined, is a disorder that makes people feel frightened even when they aren't in danger. Physiologically, it is characterized by the body's failure to resume to normal functioning after a crisis has passed. People with PTSD have difficulty regulating their emotions and knowing what they are feeling. For many reasons that are probably already obvious, it affects their offspring and the entire community. Symptoms of PTSD can be grouped into three categories: *re-experiencing symptoms, hyperarousal symptoms and avoidance symptoms.*[20]

As a trauma therapist, of course I work with people who have been diagnosed with PTSD. But on a much grander scale, and far beyond PTSD, I find myself working with people who don't consider themselves survivors of trauma at all. Yet they struggle in relationships and experience negative self-limiting beliefs that somehow keep them falling short of actually thriving in their lives. Survival is what they are up to. Why? Because at some level they don't *feel* safe. They experience symptoms from all of the categories of PTSD, just not to the degree that keeps them from functioning. Looking deeper, it seems quite possible that trauma is a condition that plagues many of us even if we don't have a diagnosis, even if we don't think we've had it "that bad." Recognizing the signs of trauma, and knowing what trauma actually does to the body, is an important part of caring for ourselves, identifying the effects of developmental trauma, and understanding others who have been affected.

So let's return to the idea of trauma, which is the body's response to a threat. The response (set of bodily responses) in and of itself is adaptive. What makes it problematic is when the body does not return to its pre-threat state after the threat has passed. What we are talking about here is a chronic failure to recover from survived threat. It's as if a circuit blows and for some reason, the system can't return to business as usual.

What constitutes the kind of threat that is so intense that it short-circuits the system? The event or set of circumstances that triggers PTSD can vary from person to person, and depends on a combination of so many things including age, temperament, birth order, stage of development, knowledge and understanding, past experiences, and felt support. The list could go on and on.

In very broad strokes, we might say that a threat is something that makes you afraid. Elements of that scary thing could include its novelty. What I have noticed is that things that end up traumatizing people are things that the individual *had never experienced before*. Add to that, these experiences actually seemed life-threatening at the time. Such peril would include threat to one's own life and/or the life of someone close, and of course what feels threatening depends very much on how old and developed we are. But there is yet another component to the threat that makes it "significant," and it has more to do with context. What is often overlooked in trauma is the relational support available to the survivor, both before and after the terrifying event.

Karla McLaren[21] describes how event trauma parallels a tribal initiation, where a person is sent out into the world to complete a task or mission. During this mission, he or she encounters something intensely challenging.   It is so challenging, in fact, that during at least some part of the experience, the initiate is not sure whether he or she will be able to complete the mission and survive. Ultimately, he or she somehow does complete the mission and survive the ordeal, and physically returns to his or her tribe. This is where things get interesting with regard to trauma. What McLaren suggests is that with an individual who is welcomed back home with adequate support and care, receiving adequate attention, empathy, and understanding, the person is transformed. The support of such a tribe, she says, is what ushers in a more fully developed person, who is newly wedded with maturity and gifts that would not have been discovered had it not been for the initiatory experience. Trauma, as the disorder we are talking about here, she says, happens when the initiate survives his or her intense and terrifying experience and is *not* received by the tribe. For one reason or another, the cycle cannot end without the third and final stage of initiation, which is the return. And without the return, he or she cannot tell his or her story, and cannot be heard or seen. The injury that is created as a result of this fundamental deficit, along with the burden of the unresolved fear, becomes a wedge between him or her and the help and support of safe others. He or she then remains alone with the burden, and does not naturally move toward recovery and maturity. And without recovery, he or she is destined to repeat the initiatory cycle, until it can be completed.

This topic is very personal to me because as I review the literature, uncovering research that speaks to me, and finding out what others have been learning, I feel curious, deeply validated and strangely affirmed. In a way, I feel as though I were finally coming home. In gaining the language to talk about these things, which slowly, painstakingly come together into a story, I finally know there are others who understand me, that I am supported, and that I am no longer alone.

Re-Experiencing

Of the three symptom categories of PTSD, re-experiencing can be one of the most obvious, and possibly the most baffling. I've heard it countless times: *I can't believe it. How many times am I going to have to go through this before I learn? Once again, I'm involved with this woman/I have this job/I have a 'friend' who...* You know what I'm talking about. Humans naturally repeat behaviors until they feel they have gained mastery over the fearful situation, or until the trauma is healed. This tendency has been referred to as the repetition compulsion as far back as Freud. We all see this phenomenon in our lives, and must not blame ourselves for what many could perceive as self-defeating or masochistic tendencies.

In a conversation I had with my sister, Trina Brunk,[22] when we were designing a "playshop" retreat on Inner Authority a few years ago, we were casting the net very widely in thinking about how we *know* things. What inevitably came up was the type of "knowing" that happens when we meet someone, and the attraction is so strong that there is just no avoiding it. What is *that* about? Without a doubt, attraction can be a mighty motivator. It is often difficult to discern between such attraction and more grounded or rational ways of navigating our lives. So often, following such attractions ends up giving us yet another chance to live through trauma. Is the attraction actually a subconscious urge; our system's primitive ability to override reason, so that we can have another chance to live through a past traumatic experience? Whatever it is, it tends to be extremely effective at convincing us that *it* is the single path to bliss and effortlessness—the answer to all our problems forever and ever. And it often seems we have no other choice but to follow it.

Reenactment is another word for this phenomenon. Yes, there can be a very compelling tug toward re-experiencing those things that constitute trauma from the past. For one thing, reenactment, according to Clinical Professor of Neurological Surgery Michael S. Levy,[23] "can provide an opportunity to integrate and work through the terror, helplessness, and other feelings and beliefs surrounding the original trauma".[24] Like Karla McLaren says, it is the psyche's way of giving the individual another chance to re-immerse in the initiatory cycle with the potential to come out on the other side and finally be received by the tribe and thus experience the gifts and the maturity that come with the completion of an initiatory experience. Levy has broken this idea down in a very helpful way that I will draw upon in the remainder of this section.

As so many of us have seen, completion and learning are not always the natural result of reenactment. Levy points out that what often stands in the way of learning is the rigidity of our identity or defensive coping styles. And rigidity itself is one of the main contributors to re-experiencing. For instance, in attempts to avoid negative experiences from the past, a man might inadvertently adopt a style of relating that ends up causing what he is avoiding; he wants so badly to avoid being abandoned that he clings to his partner and ultimately drives her away because of what she perceives as neediness, immaturity and possessiveness. It can also appear as having a rigid sense of identity where you can only perceive of yourself as "the strong one" in a relationship. In this way, you sidestep the fearful position of shared vulnerability by picking a partner unlikely to abandon you rather than a partner you actually love, respect and admire.

Not having the skills to confidently navigate emotions is another cause for reenactment. The person with unresolved trauma can feel that he or she is making decisions based on reason, toward the best possible outcome, when unknowingly he or she is influenced by an urgent subconscious drive to avoid overwhelming feelings. According to Levy:

Trauma survivors may also be drawn to establish relationships that are similar to past significant relationships because there is comfort in familiarity. For example, a man who was emotionally abused by his aloof, distant mother ends up in a relationship with a woman with similar traits. It has been found that when animals are hyperaroused, they tend to avoid novelty and perseverate in familiar behavior regardless of the outcome. However, in states of low arousal they seek novelty and are curious. For many victims of childhood abuse, dealing with other people on an intimate basis is a high-arousal state because past relationships have been marked by terror, anxiety, and fear.[25]

Reenactments can also be caused by general ego deficits, says Levy. When people feel that they are somehow incomplete in and of themselves, or that they need another to complete them, they are likely to attract partners who will dance this familiar dance with them, yet again. "Early childhood abuse can lead to ego deficits that render an individual susceptible to both reenactments and repeated revictimization."[26]

Deep seated disturbances in identity, self-concept, and security in the world can also render individuals vulnerable to being enticed by others who resonate with and counter these

33

ego deficits. Because of early trauma, a person can feel helpless, fragile, and out of control. In turn, the person may be extremely susceptible to anyone who can take control, who can gratify dependency needs, and who can elegantly counter the individual's extreme sense of powerlessness, insecurity, and vulnerability.[27]

Dissociative defenses can also contribute to frequent reenactments. We can "not know" things that we know. We can deny what doesn't fit within our rigid schemas of how the world works.

Individuals with a history of trauma seem to minimize, block out, not see, and tolerate [...] abuse. Although this may have an adaptive value since it allows the person to tolerate the situation, simultaneously it will inhibit appropriate action, and past abuse may be reenacted.[28]

Hyperarousal

Out of the research on attachment comes a concept called intergenerational trauma, which is responsible for ruptures in attachment bonds, bonding being one of the fundamental developmental necessities of all mammal infants. Such research has implicated maternal depression during the child's first two years of life, as responsible for higher stress hormone levels in children as they move into preschool and beyond.

In fact, ample research currently suggests that the foundations of PTSD and dissociation lie in dysfunctional attachment.[29] We will talk more about dissociation in

Chapter 2. But a relationship between attachment style and subsequent development of trauma symptoms would make a lot of sense, given what we have already touched on, in terms of intimacy as a trigger, regression and the body's failure to recover from survived threat.

Without a doubt, *chronic or prolonged parental misattunement without adequate repair* represents the kind of significant threat we were talking about earlier. It is the threat experienced by babies and small children who live with a marked lack of parental attunement or misattunement, over the course of their earliest weeks, months and years, when their caregivers are addicted, depressed, mentally ill, isolated, stressed without coping mechanisms or support, and/or are traumatized themselves. When this happens, a child is vulnerable to experiencing his or her parent at his or her worst, the child is vulnerable to developing coping styles in which he or she denies his or her needs in favor of caring for and minimizing stress for the parent, and the child is vulnerable to deficiencies in physical, social and emotional inputs necessary for proper development. I will talk more about attunement in Chapter 3. Lyons-Ruth, et al. identify threat, from the point of view of an infant, to be:

> *closely related to the caregiver's affective signals and availability rather than to the actual degree of physical or survival threat inherent in the event itself. Equipped with limited behavioral and cognitive coping capacities, the infant cannot gauge the actual degree of threat. Instead, primary experiences of threat in infancy include the threat of separation from the caregiver and the threat of having little caregiver response to [...] signals of distress*[30].

Attachment styles between babies and their parents have been studied in great depth for the past several decades and the literature identifies something quite interesting, referred to as disorganized attachment, which is directly related to both PTSD and dissociation. Apparently, disorganized children produce larger increases in the stress hormone cortisol in response to separation and reunion with their parents than children classified as securely *or* insecurely attached. Disorganized attachment resembles dissociative states in infants and young children. According to Main and Solomon:

> *These infants are experiencing low stress tolerance and [...] disorganization and disorientation reflect the fact that the infant, instead of finding a haven of safety in the relationship, is alarmed by the parent. They note that because the infant inevitably seeks the parent when alarmed, any parental behavior that directly alarms an infant should place it in an irresolvable paradox in which it can neither approach, shift its attention, or flee. At the most basic level, these infants are unable to generate a coherent active coping strategy to deal with this emotional challenge.[31]*

Pete Walker talks about the feeling of abandonment babies and children can feel that can be devastating not only because of the physical sensations of the emotions produced, but because of the inability to talk about them or to be supported through them by a safe, attuned adult.

> *When children sense that no one has their back, they feel scared, miserable and disheartened. Much of the constant anxiety that adult*

survivors live in is still aching fear that comes from having been so frighteningly abandoned.[32]

Barry and Janae Weinhold explain that failure to complete bonding and separation results in behaviors they categorize as counter-dependent. The stronger the bond, they say, the easier it is for a child to become separate later on. They attribute developmental trauma to "subtle disconnects between parent and child involving the lack of, or loss of, emotional attunement."[33] They use terms such as emotional and spiritual abandonment to describe the sources of stress that children experience that constitute developmental trauma. In comparison to physical abuse or neglect, they describe developmental trauma this way:

> *With physical abandonment or neglect, people had a tangible experience that leaves them knowing "something happened." Emotional and spiritual abandonment or neglect are less concrete. They can result when a parent is physically present but emotionally absent, or when a parent neglects to support the child's emotional needs for touch, holding and comfort. These types of abandonment or neglect are more difficult to identify because they are less visible, but they can leave deep scars. [Emotional and spiritual abandonment are] harder to identify, because "nothing happened," except that the children's social and emotional needs were neglected by the significant adults in their lives.*[34]

Counter-dependent behaviors, according to the Weinholds,[35] include:

- Attempting to hide normal fears, anxieties, or insecurities from others.
- Finding it difficult to identify and/or express important feelings.
- Attempting to always "look good" and always be "right."
- Lacking trust in other people's motives.
- Feeling anxious in close, intimate relationships.
- Finding it difficult to ask for help from others when needed.
- Preferring to work alone.
- Having low tolerance for frustration, marked by temper tantrums or fits of anger when frustrated.
- Fearing being smothered or controlled by the needs of others.
- Sexualizing all nurturing touch.
- Being addicted to work, sex, activity, or exercise.
- Trouble getting close to people.
- Trouble sustaining closeness in intimate relationships.
- Viewing people as bad or wrong when you leave them or they leave you.
- Trouble feeling your feelings other than justified anger or sadness.
- Fearing other people controlling you.
- Saying no to the new ideas of others.
- Feeling constantly afraid you will make a mistake.
- Trying to be perfect and expecting others to be perfect.
- Having a strong need to be right.
- Having thick layers of muscle or fat across your shoulders, chest, or abdomen that create a kind of body armor.
- Making high demands on yourself and others.
- Tending to see people as all good or all bad, depending on how they relate to you.

- Working long hours during the week and going in to work on weekends too.
- Keeping very busy with hobbies, recreation, or other projects.
- Finding it difficult to relax and do nothing.
- Having difficulty with free play or unstructured time.

Hypervigilance is one of the signatures of trauma. As can be seen in the list above, the inability to trust, relax and feel safe are common characteristics of survivors of developmental trauma. When a child is not certain that his or her adult caretaker is in a position to keep him or her safe or attune to his or her needs, the child is correct in feeling that all is not right in the world. For this child, an over-aroused sympathetic nervous system drives him or her to remain hypervigilant. His or her temperament becomes one of incessant, on-guard scanning of the people in the environment, in an effort to recognize, predict and avoid danger. And as Perry et al. conclude, "in the infant brain, states become traits, and so the imprinting of early relational trauma as well as dissociation, the major defense against attachment trauma, are embedded into the core structure of the evolving right brain."[36] In later life, it is common for this tendency to manifest as lack of boundaries and intense performance anxiety.

One of the things parents of disorganized infants in the attachment studies did to unknowingly contribute to attachment problems was responding to the infant with a "frightened" expression (Main & Solomon, 1986).[37],[38] Lyons-Ruth, et al., explain how this works by saying that the infant would infer that there was something threatening in the environment or that the child, himself, was threatening in some way. And while such perceived environmental threat would lead a securely attached infant to approach his parent for protection,

> The [disorganized] infant may sense the helplessness of the parent in the face of threat and demonstrate conflict about approaching him or her for protection by displaying contradictory simultaneous or sequential approach-avoidance behaviors typical of disorganized detachment. Alternatively, the parent's frightened stance may cause the child to infer that he, himself, is frightening the parent, again leading to conflict in approaching and further threatening an already frightened parent.[39]

Parental withdrawal, whether or not the parent's behavior exhibits fright or elicits fear from the infant, is characteristic of parents who were not raised with adequate affection, and are themselves operating with unresolved developmental trauma. Parental withdrawal is also associated with disorganized attachment.

> Thus, the infant's internalization of contradictory models of the self as frightened or threatening and of the parent as hostile or helpless/withdrawing can be conceptualized in terms of contradictory models that generate incompatible behavioral and mental tendencies.[40]

Parenting, as it turns out, is rife with millions of little triggers for the adult person, who, if he or she has unresolved traumas, can be sent unknowingly into hyper-aroused states for brief periods, or even for many days. When this

40

happens, adrenal hormones flow through the parent's bloodstream. And the infant or child, at a very primal level, is highly sensitive to these hormones and the parent's physiology in general.

As parents, when we are triggered, we are essentially re-living some past event, and as such we don't have sufficient attention available to allow us to take in current input from the here and now. Therefore the truth of the current situation as it could be available to us through our five senses is not taken in, and the *story* of the original trauma is reinforced, whether the facts surrounding the situation match or not. Such triggering can play out in many ways, showing up as facial expressions, reactive verbal responses, mood states, or worse. Rage is another way people can respond when they are triggered. John Lee describes rage in the following paragraph taken from *Growing Yourself Back Up*.

> *[Rage] cannot be expressed safely and harms both those on whom it is inflicted and those who inflict it. Rage is not a feeling but rather a behavior or action that a person demonstrates when they are emotionally regressing. They regress because they are afraid to feel their feelings of sadness, anger, hurt, loneliness or abandonment. In other words, anger is a grown-up emotion that we feel in the present. Rage is a behavior that we exhibit when we get stuck in feelings left over from unresolved situations and relationships from the past.* [41]

Other things that constitute threat to an infant or a child include depriving the brain of what it needs. On this list of critically necessary things, I like to include physical comfort and soothing, role models for healthy human interaction, and role models for resolving conflict. And last but not least, the permission to be who one is. Regardless of the reasons, when these needs go unmet, the consequences are predictable and natural. We can and should attribute the fallout from deficiencies in any of these areas as developmental trauma. Moreover, the research has shown that they result in chronic levels of physiological arousal and predict difficulty in relating with others in adult life.

Avoidance

Avoidance as a symptom of PTSD is easy to understand. Avoidance can protect a person from getting hurt again. If I'm in a near-fatal accident, I may not be so eager to get into a car again. At least until the trauma is addressed in some way. Even if I'm tough (or determined), my body may give me signals so strong when I attempt to get into the car, I cannot follow through. I am compelled to stay home, or to choose other ways to get around for a while. Avoidance can also be one of those things that survivors of trauma have to deal with on a day-to-day basis. For instance, phobias that develop after a rape can generalize to all men, which would cause a victim to stay home in order to avoid running into someone who is going to trigger those memories and feelings again. One client puts it this way: "People with trauma struggle with avoidance on a daily basis, which only causes further disconnect and dissociation. Just thinking about the energy I have used to avoid certain things, places and situations that trigger trauma for me or make me truly uncomfortable (my avoidance tendencies), causes me so much anxiety but it also creates barriers between me and what I really want. It also has contributed to my parenting. And now I can recognize my avoidance issues in some of my children."[42]

How this relates to our topic of undiagnosed trauma and its impact on intimacy and attachment is that certain physiological states that children resort to in response to chronic or acute stress predispose them to very powerful defenses against re-experiencing vulnerability in interpersonal relations later in life. And this physiological state, referred to here as degrees of *hypo*arousal, becomes an ingrained defense, which the child begins to use habitually, even at lower levels of stress. While still children, they use this defense to habitually shut themselves down to the external relational environment, and do not develop along the normal social or emotional paths that lead to feelings of safety and comfort in interpersonal interactions. And then they go on to draw people and circumstances into their lives through which the story will inevitably repeat. Schore, et al. goes so far as to say that the detachment that results becomes an "attractor" state:[43]

> *Intimate social relationships are habitually appraised at a nonconscious level to be dangerous, because these contexts are always potential triggers of "vehement emotions." The avoidance of emotional connections, especially those containing novel and more complex affective information, prevents emotional learning, which in turn precludes any advances of right brain emotional intelligence (Schore, 2001a) or what Janet calls an "enlargement" of personality.[44]*

Complex Post Traumatic Stress Disorder (CPTSD)

Complex trauma, as we have already discussed, is inherently relational. It stems from a child's adaptations to stressors in early life, and has implications in areas of relationship and physical as well as mental health. Pete Walker does an excellent job developing the idea of CPTSD and essentially opened a door for me to see my own childhood experience differently. Complex trauma, or CPTSD, is the result of profound emotional abandonment during childhood. I'd like to invite you to go back and read that sentence again. Thinking of oneself as having experienced emotional abandonment does not necessitate making our parents bad or wrong. It does involve opening the mind and the heart to being present for the self at a particular moment in time that has left an imprint below the level of awareness but which tends to surface when we are triggered. I was not the direct *target* of what Walker describes below as a stressful environment in which to grow up. But someone else very close to me was.

> *Ongoing assault with critical words systematically destroys our self-esteem and replaces it with a toxic inner critic that incessantly judges us as defective. Even worse, words that are emotionally poisoned with contempt infuse the child with fear and toxic shame [...] Unrelenting criticism, especially when it is ground in with parental rage and scorn, is so injurious that it changes the structure of the child's brain [...] Repeated messages of disapproval are internalized and adopted by the child, who eventually repeats them over and over to himself.[45]*

Learning about CPTSD helped me be compassionate with the self I was as I watched and listened to my older sister being disciplined. And to better understand her, as well. She was very strong-willed, and my parents were raised in an age where there was possibly even more confusion about parenting than there is today. Witnessing my sister trigger all of my parents' unresolved fear and trauma produced in me the desire to comply, to please, and to blend in.

So much of this happens below the level of our consciousness that it is really hard to assess the damages without some distance. Having spent a great deal of time with my older sister in the past two years, I've experienced some events with her where I became dissociated, or unknowingly entered emotional flashbacks, which Walker describes as being the most noticeable and characteristic feature of CPTSD. Unlike PTSD, emotional flashbacks do not typically have a visual component. I ultimately realized I was dissociated from the present and took steps to return to the here and now, communicating things I needed to communicate with my sister, and adjusting power imbalances that had happened between us. Looking back over my life, I am still trying to sort out what chapters were conscious, and what parts were dissociated. I have no doubt that my choice in partners was affected by CPTSD. For whatever reason, we resonate with, or are attracted to in some way, people and situations who/which will ultimately give us the opportunity to see these unprocessed memories in "living color," so that we can finally experience them on a *conscious* level. The good news is that when we can put them into words, we can deal with them. Here is Pete Walker on emotional flashbacks.

> *Emotional flashbacks are sudden and often prolonged regressions to the overwhelming*

feeling-states of being an abused/abandoned child. These feeling states can include overwhelming fear, shame, alienation, rage, grief and depression. They also include unnecessary triggering of our fight/flight instincts.

It is important to state here that emotional flashbacks, like most things in life, are not all-or-none. Flashbacks can range in intensity from subtle to horrific. They can also vary in duration ranging from moments to weeks on end where they devolve into what many therapists call a regression.[46]

What happens that makes emotional flashbacks difficult to deal with is that we don't realize we're dealing with a flashback. We just think we're trapped in some temporary unexplainable crisis, and if we just keep our heads about us, we will get through it. This is partly true, but there is so much more to it. And so much can be gained from studying our flashbacks and identifying the components of the present situation that resemble the unresolved memories from the past. The events that happened in the past may have actually only lasted for minutes, but they remain frozen in their original form until they are appropriately dealt with. Until they are dealt with, they remain in the state we were referring to earlier as emotional cysts.

Understandably, it takes a lot of courage to say, *"This happened to me,"* without feeling excessively self-indulgent, reckless or irresponsible. After all, we're a respectable family, and why would I bring this up anyway, since I've obviously survived and not done too poorly at that. Why not just let sleeping dogs lie? That is a compelling argument indeed, and I am acknowledging its appropriateness in some circumstances, but not those in which *your* voice is silenced at the expense of your recovery. In families of verbal and emotional violence and abandonment, it is common to minimize or deny the hurt, pain, and toxicity of the abuse. But it is time to shine the light of awareness on our stories so that we can heal and move on. Walker explains it this way:

> *The degree of recovery matches the degree to which a survivor's story is complete, coherent, and emotionally congruent and told from a self-sympathetic perspective [...] a narrative that highlights the role of emotional neglect in describing what one has suffered and what one continues to deal with.*[47]

So while it might seem like senseless self-indulgence, betrayal of your parents, or wallowing in self-pity, telling your story is the first step toward recovery from complex or developmental trauma. The more you identify and name the damage, the more you know what to fix. This book, besides being my attempt to bring the topic to you, is me rescuing my inner child from the loneliness of never feeling safe to be seen or heard. The story in the box at the end of this chapter is that of my older sister, Tracy. In a way, my sister and I conspired to keep this story untold so as to avoid dwelling on the negative or disparaging our parents. But without telling her story, mine remains untold as well.

Effects of Stress and Trauma on the Brain

Stress, in the form of childhood neglect and abuse, has a huge impact on brain development. In this section, I will talk about some basic brain structures and what they do under extreme stress and then how extreme stress affects memory storage.

The Smoke Detector, The Cook & The Watchtower

The things that distinguish the traumatized brain, according to Bessel van der Kolk, can be summarized by three points.[48] The organism's threat perception is enhanced, the filtering system gets messed up, and the self-sensing system gets blunted. He describes the function of the affected regions of the brain by using three easy-to-remember metaphors:

The **Smoke Detector** consists of the amygdala. The Smoke Detector is the region responsible for threat perception. This is the part of the brain that makes you afraid. The Smoke Detector works below awareness, continually scanning the environment. Therefore, it is designed to kick in without our needing to tell it to through conscious input.

The **Cook** consists of the thalamus. The Cook is continually cooking and stirring information as it comes in from the senses. It serves as a filtering system between what we are taking in with our senses and our reactions to it. Extreme stress or trauma can make the thalamus goes offline, and when it does, we get a disconnect between the outer mantle of the brain (the cortex) and the thalamus. We get no more sensory information from the body and we end up with unprocessed memories (more on this later).

The **Watchtower** consists of the dorsolateral prefrontal cortex and the medial prefrontal cortex. The Watchtower is the one area of the brain that has the function of allowing us to have some distance from our emotional selves. From here arises our ability to distinguish, *That was* then, *this is* now. *I am feeling this feeling, but* I am not *this feeling*. It is also the area responsible for self experience, for looking inward and noticing what is happening in our bodies. This is the interface that we can develop through mindfulness in order to use information from our bodies to recognize when we are in need of a time-out to reboot the system, to regroup and attend to the care of the machine. In van der Kolk's words, "The Watchtower is the only part of the conscious brain that has any control over the primitive organism."[49]

Two huge chemical reactions characterize the traumatized brain. One is the acute secretion of cortisol, and the other is high levels of adrenaline. Adrenaline helps us remember details that could help us stay safe in the future, by increasing the encoding of implicit memory (more of this in the next section). Cortisol blocks the normal activity of the hippocampus, which integrates memory. By doing so, it helps put a brake on the stress system/the stress response, but extends periods of neurotoxic cortisol release.

Trauma or extreme stress can flip a switch in the brain so that parts of it go offline. These include the Cook (the thalamus), the Watchtower (the cortex) and Broca's Area, the region responsible for narrative speech. This is what Lee was talking about when he described regression. The system experiences the event as happening *now*, and the body behaves as if trauma *were* happening now. And our ability to sense the body is blunted, so none of these things are completely apparent to us. All of this happens below our awareness through the production and release of cortisol and adrenaline in response to the Smoke Detector's (the amygdala's) perception of threat.

Memory

Another way of looking at trauma is that *an unprocessed memory is essentially keeping the stress response alive.*

Scholars and researchers on trauma have broken down memory into several different types. The first division is into *explicit memory* and *implicit memory*. Recall what you ate yesterday. Chances are, you can think back and tell me, using words, something about what you ate. This is explicit memory. For simplicity, let's say it is stored on the left side of the brain, along with language and logic. Explicit memory stored from childhood can actually change over time, with additional input, maturity, and therapy.

Implicit memory, on the other hand is the raw, sensory information that one has about a particular event. It might be the juiciness of the peach I felt in my mouth, or the crunch of an apple. It might be the smell of coffee that still lingers in my mind from this morning's breakfast, or the good feeling I had because I shared breakfast with someone special. Again, for the sake of simplicity, let's say that implicit memory is stored on the right side of the brain, along with emotions, creativity and intuition.

We can break down implicit memories further still, into emotional memories and procedural memories. *Emotional memories* are those feelings we get that let us know something significant has happened. They are designed to get our attention. In contrast, *procedural memories* are what the body does automatically: stiffen, fight, flee, freeze. So it is quite possible to have a procedural memory and be consciously unaware of it. Though a facial or postural expression is visible to others and communicates our emotional state, if we are dissociated from our bodies, we will have limited or no awareness of it. Dan Siegel, psychiatrist and Harvard-trained clinical professor of psychiatry at the UCLA School of Medicine, describes procedural memory as "the memory for [a particular] action, trying or wanting to run but not being able to take that action."[50] Under certain circumstances, these memories (emotional and procedural) spontaneously emerge. Thus, we could also refer to them as automatic responses. If they are indeed memories, we should probably go so far as to call them *body memories*. The body certainly remembers what happened in the past, particularly if the memory was traumatic, and the trauma has not been properly resolved.

Trauma involves a release of hormones that intensifies the encoding of implicit memory. Under normal circumstances, the information we take in, in its original form (body sensation, images, smells, tastes, visceral experience) is processed during the subsequent hours and days, and particularly while we sleep, and sorted, so that whatever is not deemed important to survival is discarded and the rest is stored in the form of explicit memory. If the experience was traumatic, this processing does not take place, and the implicit memory remains frozen on the right side of the brain in its original form. In other words, as stress hormones increase, the senses take in as much sensory information as they can, and this input is stored as implicit, raw data that will be available for use in the future to help ensure survival. According to Siegel, "Trauma impairs the brain's memory systems by blocking the integrative role of the hippocampus to take implicit puzzle pieces and weave them together into explicit memory."[51]

We are also learning that memory is being constantly updated. Memories are not static. None of our traumatic memories can resolve, however, until the implicit memory changes. And this means revisiting those implicit memories in one way or another, whether it is through re-experiencing and learning on your own, or with the help of an experienced guide or therapist. Eye Movement Desensitization and Reprocessing (EMDR) is one way of jump-starting the body's ability to process memories from implicit to explicit. There are a good number of other effective body-inclusive therapies available as well. But it is important to keep in mind that any effective trauma therapy will involve the body, mindfulness and the senses.

PARENTS' UNRESOLVED TRAUMA, PASSED DOWN

"I don't really know which Daddy is going to come home—the Fixer or the Scary Dad."

Some parents can shower love on babies. But as soon as the child begins toddling around and expressing a will of her own, they become severely punishing and rejecting. This is what happened to Tracy whose mother was very often critical, controlling, and a perfectionist. And since Tracy was the firstborn, she was regularly the target of scrutiny, oppression and violence.

Everyone knew Tracy had a genius-level IQ, even before she went to kindergarten. She remembers creating secret worlds and languages when she was a child. She would escape into the woods with her dog, Brownie, and she would read everything she could get her hands on. It hasn't been until recently that she has been willing to set the denial aside and *let herself know* what she was escaping from. As a newborn, and a 2-year-old, she didn't understand why her father was so angry, why the two of them clashed so often and so fiercely. Her 12-year-old self didn't know that she was serving the family's need for a scapegoat when her father reached back and smacked *"whoever he could reach."* It would not have been healthy then, or "mature" now, to acknowledge that he would not have smacked her sister, who played the role of "the good one," the one who brown-nosed her way into their parents' hearts. Her 14-year-old self didn't realize it was traumatizing when he would assault her with his words. But it was.

Tracy would recount her story of abuse in bits and pieces that would slide out sideways when she wasn't careful, but more often, she would polish it, and make it into a tribute to her parents' love, hard work and dedication. But the telling of the real story is not only important to her recovery, but also to mine, because I learned how to conduct my life by watching her as she was abused. Stories such as these may take some time to reconstruct in a complete way. But when they are finished, they have a calm voice, with some safe distance, with perspective, with 100 percent compassion for the children that we were.

Besides being creative, Tracy was a very hard worker, too. So she took these traits and used them to build an illustrious career, marked by awards and recognition and many admirers and followers.[52] But she never really did measure up by her own impossible standards. In fact, she had a harsh, cruel, inner critic who in times of doubt or vulnerability would shoot her down, causing her to feel that what she was doing would never be good enough. In telling part of her healing story, here is an excerpt of Tracy's process:

> *I keep coming back to what it is I need to do, what I need to be, in order to be loved... and what love looks like when it comes my way. It's not soft and*

*fuzzy, it's got sharp edges and can be dangerous.
It's righteous, though, and Godly, and very
disciplined. So that's how I need to be in order to be
loved. I need to measure up. I need to work hard,
and well. No daydreaming. No lollygagging. No
reading the labels on the cereal boxes... and
definitely no talking back. If I even dared to dream
up a comeback to match that sarcasm.... But I
couldn't. It would be slapped right out of my mouth.*

What Tracy learned through her parents' unresolved trauma
was that she would need to measure up to certain standards
in order to be loved. She was also the target of quite a bit of
contempt and ridicule. Tracy was a storyteller though, and
so she wove versions of her childhood that looked like *The
Waltons*, or *Little House on the Prairie*. It wasn't until she
looked back at her interactions with her bosses and
professors that she could begin to see the patterns.

*No wonder I chose a profession in which my
mentors were harsh, largely male and largely
verbally abusive. Schneller the Yeller. He was my
favorite. He ridiculed us publicly, and often. "You
didn't ASK????" he would demand in a tone that
would turn heads all around the newsroom. "WHY
didn't you ask????" A question for which there was
no answer. Only to hang one's head and feel
profound shame. A shame that goes all the way
back to the very beginning, or very close to the
beginning.*

Perhaps it was the lack of communication, negotiation, and
emotional intelligence modeled in her home growing up, or
the belief that she adopted early on that nothing was really

worth anything unless one had to struggle and suffer a great deal in order to obtain it—or a combination of both—that shaped Tracy's tendencies in relationships.

> *So I itched for a challenge…. And I found it. On the dance floor, at Sam's Burger Joint. It came in the form of someone who needed my help. He chose me as his mentor and I fell in love with him for reasons I can't quite recall. What I remember now is that it was a new crisis every day with him; I remember leaving the newsroom on a regular basis to have long conversations with him on my cell phone in the hall because he was in a crisis. I wanted to be a hand up to him, but he ended up pulling me down into a very dark place, in the most abusive and dysfunctional relationship of my life, for two years.*

In middle age now, Tracy knows that there are certain unexplained patterns in her life that she feels she has no control over. And though she has worked extensively to connect in healthy ways with other people and herself, she notices an undeniable set of factors that point to developmental arrests that she does not know exactly what to do with. The idea of having played the role of the scapegoat of the family was something that would have never occurred to Tracy on her own. She was too willing to blame herself for anything negative that was happening to her. Hold someone else responsible? Not likely. She was still too much in denial about what had happened to her as a child, and too accustomed to abusing herself from the inside. In her adult life, Tracy invested a great deal in learning how to communicate effectively, how to maintain emotional balance, all the while making a difference in the world using her skills and passion. Part of her recovery has involved spiritual practices, compassion, and magnanimity.

Her father, as it turns out, was suffering from a great deal of stress, some intermittent depression, and quite a bit of ambivalence about having a daughter so early in his marriage. Some days he would be just the Daddy any child would want. He went to work and provided money to pay the bills and buy the groceries. He might also take you swimming, or camping, or on a ride on his motorcycle. And Daddy could fix things, and often did. Sometimes, though, "when Daddy would come home he would be angry and scary." Understandably, not knowing which one was going to show up had a profound impact on her developing psyche.

> *My difficulties in making decisions—stemming from a deficit in knowing what I want, something I've struggled with my whole life—may come from this dynamic. Waiting for my daddy the fixer to come home and fix things. But I don't really know which Daddy is going to come home—the fixer or the scary Dad.*

Also, due to the emotional fragility of her parents, she was not allowed to express or explore the world of emotions. "Stop crying or I'll give you something to cry about," was commonly heard in the home. And so in order to cope, Tracy developed automatic ways of responding to stress in her home and school life. According to Walker's 4F system, her primary style of sympathetic activation was flight (flights of fantasy, reading, exploring nature) and when flight was not an option, she resorted to a fighting stance.

Unlucky for her, because getting angry back in her family was a capital crime that would elicit the most savage retaliation. "I'll knock you from here to kingdom come," is a phrase that rings through my memory—not as a threat to me, but to someone in my close proximity. Not to mention, "What are you laughing at? Wipe that smile off your face." These were things that Tracy was told, no doubt in our parents' worst moments. But they are clear examples of violence; the slaughtering of willfulness and emotional expression.

Chapter 2 - Dissociation

I wake up one morning with this *knowing*—this understanding about what is happening when people dissociate. I sit bolt upright, and I suddenly understand. And I have this incredible, timeless image in my mind. It is of two ancient, statue-like figures, who look like they could be made of stone because they're mottled gray and weathered and softened with time, but they move with slow, deliberate action. One is male, the other is female. They stand in the sea, water coming up to somewhere below the waist. Their job is to assist passing ships that may be having trouble navigating, or staying upright in a turbulent sea.

I see. This is where we go when we dissociate—that is, when we aren't consciously living in *our* bodies. I associate this with times I've driven home on automatic pilot, clearly not noticing the other cars, the street signs, the Walgreens on the corner, or making decisions about which way to turn, which route to take, because it's an action I've taken so many times that I no longer need to be consciously present to perform it. Or when I get ready to step out of the shower and can't remember whether I actually rinsed the conditioner out of my hair. Where exactly was I during that time in the shower? Or at least where was my consciousness? The dream indicates these ancient figures as the "place" we go when we're not fully embodied, for whatever reason. Our awareness goes out and serves another cause, helping wayfaring sea folk in their journeys; keeping people safe. It's an honorable activity, actually. Not problematic, as one might think when looking back over their lives and thinking of the times they weren't quite "there," or when they notice someone else falling into a pattern of mindlessness.

And as a therapist I see another dimension of this understanding that has to do with something I've heard referred to as being "triggered." A person experiences something upsetting—usually something that feels very similar to some aspect of an unresolved childhood memory. It's a fairly regular phenomenon as I look over the course of my life. It's like a program that runs when the adrenalin is flowing and I am catapulted out of the here and now. I have an emotional response that is way out of proportion to the immediate situation, and rather than respond in a mature, thoughtful way, I slide into a groove that is familiar—so familiar that my conscious mind is not needed. It goes out to sea—to right troubled ships.

So leaving the body at this or any time is not necessarily a *bad* thing. It's neutral in the sense that I am accounted for, and I'm doing something that could even be seen as honorable. But the catch is, that I am not present or available in the moment, in my body, to choose a different response, or to pursue a new, more creative or empowered solution. Instead, I follow the well-worn groove, doing what I have always done in such situations. My conscious mind is not required. In fact, my conscious mind is more comfortably somewhere else. Absent, while I go through the motions once more, and generally speaking, doing things I'll have to deal with later. In the now, choices are being made for me, and made by me, by default as a result of my "not being all there."

There is a huge shroud of mystery surrounding dissociation—at least in the media and what I hear on the street. Among the general public, it's a word that sounds more like a diagnosis, with implications suggesting something freaky or freakish, but even more commonly deferred to the medical establishment—or the entertainment industry—to define, through clinical charts, manuals and scripts, or art or sensationalism, depending on your position in the world. And while separation from the body is an ingenious way of coping in situations where we have no control over our environment, it can become a default mode in situations where we actually can make empowered and creative choices that better serve us and the world around us. The mistake we are making is in thinking of dissociation as something that happens to severely damaged others, when in fact it is quite common and could even be happening to—God forbid—me.

While the tranquil scene of the stone sea people I described above helps lend a compassionate, accepting attitude toward dissociation, the fact of the matter remains: Dissociation is a byproduct of stress and trauma, particularly as it shows up in relational trauma. Dissociation is the state of mind that is triggered when the Smoke Detector identifies something in the current environment that harks back to that unresolved memory. It's the state of mind that happens when the primitive parts of the brain decide to disconnect the Cook and the Watchtower and launch into the physically aroused defensive response that has become automatic and reflexive. Wendy T. Behary, LCSW, in her book, *Disarming the Narcissist*, refers to this as the activation of schemas.

> *The emotional and physical circuits of the brain and body often disconnect from the executive, or decision-making, areas of the brain, which are responsible for distinguishing between events in the here and now versus the "there and then." The release of stress hormones when schemas are triggered short-circuits the executive areas of the brain, which usually allow for accuracy in reasoning and responsiveness. If you are operating from an implicit state of "there and then," your reactions and decision-making can be influenced by events and emotions of the past, rather than by what is happening in the present. And worst of all, you don't even realize it because it happens behind the scenes, outside of your awareness.*[53]

Dissociation has been defined in the *Diagnostic and Statistical Manual of Mental Disorders*, fourth edition (DSM-IV), published by the American Psychiatric Association as "a disruption in the usually integrated functions of consciousness" and described as "a protective activation of altered states of consciousness in reaction to overwhelming psychological trauma."[54]

According to the DSM-IV, a traumatic event involves threat to the physical integrity of oneself or another person. The World Health Organization[55] defined dissociation as: "a partial or incomplete loss of the normal integration between memories of the past, awareness of identity and immediate sensations, and control of body movements." According to Spiegel and Cardena,[56] dissociation is "a structured separation of mental processes (e.g., thoughts, emotions, conation, memory, and identity) that are ordinarily integrated."

According to Ruth Lanius,[57] a physician and professor of psychiatry at the University of Western Ontario, dissociation is a very broad term and can refer to a number of things. She describes dissociation as providing "an escape when no actual escape is possible. It provides a mental escape from intense experience, from intense emotions, and from intense memories."

In her 2014 National Institute for the Clinical Application of Behavioral Medicine (NICABM) interview with Ruth Buczynski, Lanius mentions four basic types of dissociation, which are dissociative flashbacks, dissociative amnesia, depersonalization and fragmentation of the self.

Childhood dissociation (or hypoarousal[58]), it is said, involves numbing, avoidance, compliance and restricted affect, which, according to trauma authorities is the same pattern as adult PTSD.[59] It is a result of various things that can happen unknowingly between parents and their babies, and is probably not something we even want to technically hold anyone accountable for. But it is something we benefit from talking about so that we can learn, and avoid replaying the same scenes over and over again.

Karla McLaren says that there is actually something sacred about dissociation, that it is understood at some deep level in the psyche to be a sacred movement into initiation.

Dissociative Flashbacks

Flashbacks consist of reliving an experience and losing your connection with the present. Whether experienced by a war veteran, a survivor of childhood sexual abuse, or an adult with developmental trauma, flashbacks are, by their very nature, dissociative. Walker describes an emotional flashback in the following paragraph. Though it does not have the visual component of a more commonly conceived flashback, it is nonetheless a force to be reckoned with.

> *In a flashback, you feel little, fragile, and helpless. Everything feels too hard. Life is too scary. Being seen feels excruciatingly vulnerable. Your battery seems to be dead. In the worst flashbacks an apocalypse feels like it will imminently be upon you...When you are trapped in a flashback, you are reliving the worst emotional times of your childhood.*[60]

According to Bessel van der Kolk, flashbacks are a rich, full, implicit memory that consumes a person in the present moment. They consist of a specific event that people are aware of reliving. When an adult has a flashback, he explains, she or he sees the event happening again. However, children, or adults traumatized as children, start behaving as if the traumatic event were happening this very moment.

In a 2014 NICAB interview with Ruth Buczynski, Dr. van der Kolk talks about being on the academic and professional scene when the PTSD diagnosis was first assigned. It was a matter of maneuvering, he said, to help the veterans receive the care and treatment they so badly needed.

> *Flashbacks are important and when we created a PTSD diagnosis, we made flashbacks central— but that is not because that is the most problematic issue in traumatic stress. We have made flashbacks a primary issue because we had to convince the VA that the problems that soldiers were having were due to the war. Flashbacks connect the symptoms to a particular memory. Flashbacks are important, but, again, the flashbacks as we originally conceived of them are of specific events that people are aware of reliving.*[61]

And because of the way the brain works, the mental realization, or the awareness that this is a flashback (that what is happening now is connected to past trauma), is not available to the person during a flashback. "They could start to behave like a very frightened and enraged person," van der Kolk says, "but they might not make a connection between [what is happening now] and what happened thirty years ago."[62]

Dissociative Amnesia

Dissociative amnesia is characterized by not having any memory of a traumatic event that has happened. For example, though this was refuted by the profession for decades, many people dissociate memories of early childhood sexual abuse, which begin to impinge on conscious awareness later in life.

Depersonalization

Depersonalization or out-of-body experiences involve removing yourself from your body in order to escape pain, or to dampen the emotional intensity of terrifying emotions.

Fragmentation of the Self

Fragmentation of the self is another form of dissociation, which involves experiencing your self as fractured or divided into parts.

Structured separation of mental processes that are ordinarily integrated

Harvard-trained psychiatrist Dan Siegel, who I've already mentioned with regard to his research on memory, talks about dissociation coming from a non-integrated brain. What it looks like in children is difficulty regulating emotions, difficulty thinking clearly under stress, and difficulty in relationships. He describes dissociation and other characteristics of dissociation in the following passage.

> *Unresolved states can be dissociative and the brain fragments under certain situations—and not always is a dissociative person always dissociative, but they have the vulnerability [to dissociate]. The brain, which can work together as a system, is vulnerable to becoming fragmented.*
>
> *You see that fragmentation in psychic numbing and they [the dissociative patient] feel numb to their body; they can feel unreal; they can have memory lapses.[63]*

The five categories above give us a very basic way to talk about dissociation, and help us understand what people might be experiencing when they dissociate. This is a subject that is undoubtedly multifaceted and complex, but this is a start. Dr. Siegel noticed in the medical setting in which he received his training a tendency for doctors to see the dissociated brain as damaged, and prescribe medication. What he has come to understand through his research and work with clients is that the brain continues to be ingeniously adaptive and plastic. "The brain is not integrated," he says, "so give psychotherapy and let the [therapeutic] relationship develop the integrative fibers of this patient's brain." The negative effects of trauma and dissociation, he says, are completely treatable.

What Happened?

So I, like so many survivors of developmental trauma, grew up feeling very frightened, unequipped, and unsupported, and that something was wrong, but not really being able to describe what I was experiencing. I began to notice that the phenomenon or at least the idea of not being fully embodied began to crop up all around me. Lucky for me, I was in a position to see the faces of dissociation, as my clients and others experienced it, as a colorful and multifaceted way to think about disembodiment and in its broadest sense the ways in which it also applied to me.

Pushing my clients to identify the irrational belief that underlies the feeling inherent to their worst memory was part of my daily work, but to identify the irrational belief underlying my own feelings was a long time coming. Now, though I first experienced this "belief" without the words, I understand the belief as: *There is no comfort, relief, or protection for me.* For infants and small children, the longing for help is a profoundly powerful feeling. In fact, this longing is a normal, adaptive biological response characteristic of vulnerable young ones that has contributed to our survival. And when a child finds, for one reason or another, that they can't have what they need, they respond by disconnecting from the longing, and in doing so, they disconnect from the felt sense of their emotions. This is what *happened*. For me, disconnecting from this feeling and the discomfort of my profound unmet vulnerability set the tone for my life in the years to come.

There is no comfort, relief, or protection for me. Whew. And hallelujah. As I tell my clients, this is the hardest part. Once the belief is identified, it can be processed, discharged and turned around. As a result of this understanding—these words—I can better care for myself. I connect deeply with the felt sense in my body. I heal.

Dissociation as a Way to Cope

Truly, the image of the stone people standing in the sea may not be all that helpful for you. And when I think of it now, it's probably less important to know where I go when I'm not in my body than how it actually affects me. I think about the qualities of those timeless figures, and the deeply compelling feeling they left me with that morning. Those figures, now that I look more closely, are unquestionably service-oriented, selfless, powerful, unafraid, very large, not inclined to go about chasing things or reacting, but standing solidly doing what only they can do (in a lot of water). These are the qualities—the abilities—that are not available to me when I'm not in my body. We might say they've gone offline.

In the flashback state I behave and make choices and say things from a place of powerlessness and fear, and I do things that do not align with my higher purposes, my vision, or my desires.[64] John Lee says that one of the main reasons we don't hear people talk about regression, and I believe the same thing is true about dissociation, is that it is so prevalent in our lives.

> *It is such an integral part of our culture and our relationships that it is often mislabeled as many other things, such as neurosis and addiction, to*

67

name just two [...it] is a universal experience, touching on many areas of our lives, including relationships with parents, children, spouses, and employers.[65]

From the perspective of attachment trauma and the developing right brain, Allan N. Schore speaks to the development of dissociation as a result of not being able to match one's frightening experience with existing cognitive schemes, and the overarching function of hypoarousal: making oneself (or parts of oneself) as invisible as possible.

[...] extreme emotional arousal results in failure to integrate traumatic memories [...] The memory traces of the trauma linger as unconscious "fixed ideas" that cannot be "liquidated" [...] they continue to intrude as terrifying perceptions, obsessional preoccupations, and somatic re-experiences.

This parasympathetic dominant state of conservation-withdrawal occurs in helpless and hopeless stressful situations in which the individual becomes inhibited and strives to avoid attention in order to become "unseen" (Schore, 994, 2001b).[6667]

BEING OUTSIDE THE BODY

"I remember stepping out of my body."
"My self stepped to the left two steps
so that my body was there receiving the yelling."

"Sometimes I dissociate," Mel told me during one of our first sessions together. Having used dissociation as a way to

---

cope with repeated, painful, and unavoidable medical intrusions on her body as a very small child, she learned to separate from her physical self.

Her Master's in Religious Studies gave her a forum in which to study her experience through a broader, more universal lens. "Dissociation in industrialized societies is seen as weird and maladaptive," she says, "But I've studied it in the context of Gods and Goddesses in Africa, where people speak and act as the deity. About shamanism. It helps me understand what was happening when I was using it to cope as a child."

"I remember screaming," she told me. "I went up on the sound. I left my body on the sound of my voice." As she grew up, Mel knew how to avoid pain by leaving her body. For her, it is just another way to use her gifts and sensitivities. She has, however, begun to make a connection between leaving her body and stress. As she gets to know herself, and understand her needs better, she can use this as a signal that she is experiencing stress, and take steps to rearrange her life in ways that effectively reduce it. The extraordinary circumstances of her early life shaped and molded her mind to individuate very early, but with a solidness of existential peace and serenity that seems to sidestep many of the negative effects of dissociation and early childhood trauma. What follows are Mel's words.

What my childhood illness taught me is that I am alone— that I alone can save myself. I have struggled with this in one form or another for most of my life, and it has been a boon to me and a challenge.

I was born with a slight mutation of my ureter that meant I had frequent UTIs. My parents discovered the condition when I was barely a year old and I had a very high fever that didn't respond to treatment. After that, the doctors told them that I would probably grow out of it—but that meant that my condition had to be monitored and I had to receive regular treatments for UTIs and semi-regular invasive x-ray procedures. For most of my young life, I was in pain and I didn't know that most people did not experience that pain. My mom had to try hard to get me to drink water, because I knew it would lead to pain, and I had to take regular antibiotics in pill form, which I hated and which made me retch.

When I was 7, I had surgery to correct the kink in my ureter. I remember waking up from surgery and being in such intense pain that I could barely think. I had a pain button next to my hand to push to bring a nurse to give me pain meds—she showed up and injected pain meds into my thighs. I had needle tracks in my thighs when I was 7.

I remember clearly seeing my mom fast asleep beside my hospital bed on one of those sleepless nights. I was in so much pain, but I didn't want to wake her—she was so worried about me, so sensitive to my pain. So I remember asking myself, "How long can I deal with the pain before pushing the button to get the nurse to come, who will wake up my mom?"

When you think things like that, you know you are truly alone in the world. No one else can make that decision but you. Alone, with my pain, I knew that I was enough—I was strong enough to make that decision, and I could be what I needed for myself. If I had the power to wait, dealing with the pain until a little later, just a little later, I could do anything for myself, I could take care of myself. I could be strong enough. And I have believed that all of my life.

Depending on myself in this way means that I have been able to be enough—be sufficient, care for myself, for most of my life. I am full of capability, am full of potential, I am the master of my action. But it is hard for me to ask for and accept help. I have been to the depth of my being, and I have learned that I am enough and more than enough for the people around me. It is easy for me to give because I know that I will always be taken care of—by me.

This great gift is not without its cost. I too easily rely on my own resources to solve my problems, when I would have a richer life by reaching out to others for help. There's a part of me that doesn't believe anyone will really, truly be there for me when everything has become painful, when the world is full of pain. But I will still do my best to protect you from pain if I can see a way to protect you, and it is in my power to provide it. I will cut my dinner in half if you need it, because I know that I will always have enough."

Chapter 3 - Parenting

Children swim in their parents' unconscious stuff. Whatever parents have not dealt with, looked at, acknowledged, or healed, children act out, feel, sense, know. It's incredible. And we all, at times, have unruly little children inside us. So whether we have flesh-and-blood children in our lives, or we are responsible only for caring for ourselves, parenting is something we can benefit from knowing how to do a little bit better.

No doubt, we've all seen it done badly. Just walk into a grocery store or Wal-Mart. At the very foundations of parenting, the adult needs to have a grounded presence. And beyond that, a whole village of support. From that kind of place, an adult caretaker might generally be able to remain attuned enough to interact well with a child and avoid regressing or going into unconscious auto-pilot.

The attitude children need from their adults as they grow has to do with flexibility and openness balanced with a strong enough sense of self and one's own limits, along with a healthy curiosity about who this child is. Toward him or herself, the adult needs to have a similar curiosity. Why does a particular behavior occur; why is this feeling felt, decision made, value cherished, attitude carried, priority demonstrated? To the extent that any parent (or person) fails to explore who they are, or lacks a sense of a grounded, resourced self, the environment they create around them becomes a sea of unconscious reactions, re-enactments, emotional flashbacks, and regressions. Think about that. A child adrift in a sea of his or her parents' unconscious "stuff."

David Wallin is a therapist who talks about how good therapy actually carries out the same functions as good-enough parenting, and how the therapeutic relationship itself is more important than therapeutic techniques or strategies a therapist might use with a client. He is a pioneer in using transference and countertransference to help his patients bring their unconscious stuff to the surface during sessions. In his interview with Randall Wyatt and Victor Yalom, he says:

> *In therapy, dissociated experience is often an experience the patient can't put into words, or thoughts or feelings. My attention often is on what is being evoked in me, because I think what people can't own or articulate, they often evoke in others. I've also got my attention on what's being enacted between me and the patient, since that's another way in which dissociated experience gets expressed.*[68]

Consider the dynamic that emerges between two parents, the synergy of their combined unresolved trauma, and the resulting culture that their union creates. What that can seem like to a child, let's say for instance a 14-year-old, is an untenable and chaotic mess of contradictions (which he or she is correct in questioning and pushing against).

But back to parents who are chronically operating in a state of auto-pilot or triggered-ness. Have you seen that parent who compulsively shushes her child? A parent who shames her child for asking a question or reaching out to touch something interesting? I'm thinking about a particular parent who herself has suffered touch starvation in childhood, who adopts a religion that validates and affirms her fear of touch and the reactions of her body to touch. Maybe it's a parent who carries a memory of having seen her parents struggling as powerless victims through some great injustice as a young child just learning about language and the world. Maybe hearing her parents trying to make sense if the situation, talking about how unjustly they have been treated, and their assessment of the situation, that could filter down to the child as myriad lessons that she then internalizes. Since children are programmed to notice and absorb virtually everything their caretakers do, they are continually absorbing conclusions with their limited understanding about how the world works. Any particular moment might be one in which she senses from the parent that she is a burden or that the world is not a safe place. Or both.

A child feels the pain and suffering of the others around her. She knows when her caretakers are stressed, and she listens for important cues. From watching how the adults deal with the situation, and listening to them talk, she begins to make her own sense of the situation. Because of the intensity of the emotions of the adults responding to the unjust situation (along with the apparent helplessness of her parents), an imprint is made. The child internalizes what is stored as an unconscious belief, and until this belief is consciously examined, it has a very strong impact on her attitudes, choices and opinions.

As an adult, this information isn't necessarily available to her like her birthdate or where she parked her car, but it is sure to show up when the dynamic in question is on the table. Beliefs I have personally been unearthing along this vein are, *Men can't be trusted; we're better off without them. There are good people and bad people in this world. Good people give and give; bad people only receive.*

Let's take, for a moment, *There are good people and bad people in this world. Good people give and give; bad people only receive.* Such an imprint causes a woman to feel good and safe about giving in her relationships, but to avoid and react unconsciously to the idea of receiving. For her, it is not safe to receive. First, she avoids being perceived as that person who receives. Secondly, she reacts when one of her children appears to be too comfortable receiving what others want to give. In a million little ways, she models deflecting the gifts of others (whether they are compliments, gratitudes, or tangible gifts, large or small); she models the correctness of not taking. Below the level of consciousness, this parent believes *Receiving is bad or somehow dangerous.* At an unexamined level, the decision to *not be a person who receives* becomes a powerful motivator for this parent's values and discipline with her children. And besides modeling this behavior, she will do all she can to shape her child's behaviors to match her own unexamined belief.

I think about the kinds of things parents can mistakenly use to guide their children's behaviors and values. A parent who as a child was often shamed indiscriminately, and his caregivers were not specific or consistent about the kinds of behaviors that were and were not acceptable or why, will become triggered in situations where his child begins to look around and react in a novel environment. In such a situation, the parent's fear that his child is misbehaving can be such a powerful trigger. In that moment, the adult is flooded with fear that his child is thoughtless, selfish, or inconveniencing someone, regardless of the reality of the current situation (but the fear is triggered below conscious awareness, so he doesn't realize he is triggered or afraid). When the parent is triggered, remember, he is not capable of assessing the information from the present; he is immersed in the emotional memory of being shamed by his own parent, and is revisited by the immensity of the imprint of the values and beliefs that he adopted from *his* triggered, unconscious parent. As a bystander in the check-out aisle, I might see this response as a knee-jerk reaction by the parent. A look, a slap, a word. A lecture. When this happens, the parent has lapsed into the well-worn groove of an emotional flashback. He may be repeating the lecture he heard when he was a child, and in the moment, he *feels* extreme urgency to convey the importance of this message to his child without engaging discernment because there is a temporary disconnect in the wiring of his brain. The moment passes, the parent returns to his senses, and the value has been passed to yet another generation without any conscious thought about its usefulness or appropriateness to the child: *It's not okay to misbehave* (ask for what I want, question authority, make noise, complain, make my dad unhappy, etc.).

HEALTHY INDIVIDUATION AND THE EMERGENCE OF SELF

(14-year-old rancor and disdain)

No fourteen-year-old should be rewarded for being

indistinguishable from her mother. Being as attuned to my mother as I was, I easily picked up her unspoken (probably unconscious) expectations of me, which I interpreted to go something like this: *You should know what I would prefer. You should know what I know. You should do it the way I would do it. When the job is done, it should be done the way I would have done it.* And the kicker, *You should be happy about all this.* Since none of this was ever directly spoken, it was never clear that the intensity of the situation had come about because of a lack of boundaries, or that there was the possibility of a yawning virtual chasm between what I knew and wanted and what she knew and wanted. Enmeshed, we aimed to operate pretty much like a single organism.

All of this came flooding back to me in a recent house-sitting arrangement, when I at first enjoyed the house and living in and caring for it. When it was time for the homeowner to return, and I started to prepare the house, I caught myself putting an inordinate amount of energy into every small detail I could conceivably imagine. Certain things about how the homeowner had been communicating with me in those days prior to her arrival triggered memories of being 14 years old, and feeling distinctly the difference between home when Mom was there and home when she wasn't. Interestingly, part of this house-sitting gig had me sharing the house with the homeowner for a number of days between legs of her travel plans. As I worked through the emotions, and made my way out of the re-enactment, I realized the extent to which my mother and I had not properly individuated.   I had been referred to as my mother's right arm, and I was so good at supporting her that it was often hard to know what I might have been doing if I had felt that some significant portion of my time actually belonged to me. In the role of my mother's right arm, I would strive to prevent or defuse her anger, and sometimes even get her approval. Having this role affirmed me in important ways, and it became a vital part of my identity.

These days, from an increasingly differentiated perspective, when I notice myself reacting emotionally, I can look at what another person is doing and saying and think to myself, *Hmmm. Well isn't that interesting?* But when you are firmly situated in a particular role, or immersed deep within the emotional re-experiencing of the original situation, there is just this vague uneasiness that descends upon you. You sense it as something disturbing but it remains hard to put your finger on. Fortunately, with willingness, care, attention, and some skill, the incident can serve as a learning moment if you can be curious and teachable.

My remaining unindividuated helped home to be a smoothly functioning place, and there was motivation, unconscious or no, on the part of my parents for me to stay "one" with them. There were already children in the family who "only thought of themselves." They were known, in a quiet sort of way, as the "bad" ones. I could read between the lines when after a row with my sister my mom would say under her breath, "There are some people in this world who give... (and then there are the *other* ones, like your sister)."

Regardless of the environment, a child will reach an age where it is natural and healthy to push toward individuation. Adolescence is one of these ages. At 14, let's say, the young teen begins to feel this as uneasiness with the status quo. I am going to ask you to indulge me while I engage my curiosity for a moment, to see what this 14-year-old might have had to say if there had been space and support for her to think and feel and be herself; if there had been a grounded adult who could have remained with her, neutral, safe and attuned. Certainly, there was something *wrong* about where she fit into the family picture.

As an extension of her mother, she had a lot of responsibility, and she enjoyed it. But she didn't have many of the rights that came with *being* her mother. She knew she didn't own the house or the things in it. She didn't own, for instance, the potato peeler, the pots or the pans, the lawn mower, or the vacuum cleaner. But they were the tools she was expected to use. She wasn't quite sure about her bed linens or her pillow. How could she know? To a certain extent, she just knew, like she knew about so many of her mother's thoughts, attitudes and opinions. And she knew because if she left, there would be some things she would and other things she would not take with her. She had heard of the idea of a hope chest, but for some reason, she didn't have one. She imagined a time when she would be able to leave her childhood home with a mixture of longing and terror. Did she own anything at all? How would she possibly manage?

Was she a guest in this house? Or was she an indentured servant? She wasn't a guest, and there seemed to be a dangerous undercurrent of debt for the privilege of being there. A debt that was too big to ever repay. She would feel it anytime she asked for something though, so she rarely ever asked. If she had asked, she might have liked to have had some money or some more clothes that weren't hand-me-downs, time she could call her own or permission to stay after school every once in a while. It was better to avoid asking, she decided. If she didn't ask, she wouldn't have to pay. In a vague place in her mind, she knew not thinking about all this was better.

If she and her mother were the same person, on the other hand—or at least part of the same unit—then it was *all* actually *hers*. As long as she lived there, she didn't need to ask to borrow or take anything. That was the unspoken trade-off.

The deal was reconciled in this way, and her teenage need to individuate went into hibernation. As for the resentment, she traded it in for entitlement, which she tucked down deep inside; this was certainly better than fighting. Remaining undifferentiated was safer and easier. She would not need to feel the vulnerability or the pain. She would not have to be reminded of her dependence on her parents for a roof over her head. She would not have to be reminded of all she should be grateful for that she had a home at all. The questions that remained unexamined, and thus unanswered, however, were: *Do I have any inherent rights? Does anything just come to me because that's the way nature intended it? Is there anything to which I am fundamentally entitled?* Love, for example. Does a child deserve unconditional love? Does a 14-year old get a voice of her own? The answer to the last question, she knew, was *no*. Not if there was no one available to listen.

According to David Wallin, in our first relationships, we learn what we can and can't think, feel, speak, or want. We actually learn, very early on, what is and is not allowed:

> *I think of dissociated experience as experience that has been ruled out on the basis of what's occurred in our early relationships. It is also a consequence of experience that is traumatic...*

My terror about being unprepared and unsupported to enter the world as an independent, capable adult, and my vulnerability about not having a voice or any inherent rights, and my confusion about not having my own self went unknown by me, therefore. As Essex, et al., explain,

> [O]ne cannot truly "know" his own experience until he is seen, recognized, and reflected on by the other. In essence then, dissociated experiences around fearful affects are not necessarily experienced and then lost or defended against, but may instead be "unthinkable" in that they have gone unrecognized by central attachment figures.[69]

It was not a conscious decision by my parents, but simply through a set of unfortunate circumstances that I was denied permission to explore who I was as a person independent of my role. I was not allowed to have power, or a voice in childhood, and when this happens to children, they naturally turn to an alternative that stays with them as they move into adulthood. According to David Richo, in his book, *Daring to Trust*, that alternative is control.

> When we were not allowed to have power in childhood—that is, denied our rightful A of allowing [a long-lasting result] can occur. [...] we might, early on, have turned to control as an alternative. Control is the poor man's version of power. We try to gain some sense of power by controlling our environment or other people. Control arises from compulsion and increases our fear; true power arises from self-trust and increases our self-esteem.[70]

Like I've tried to point out before, we're certainly not making these or any parents out to be irresponsible or wrong, though their unconscious, wound-reflective behaviors inflict acute stress if not violence, and have a profound impact on children. About this flavor of parenting that includes shaming and controlling, authors Janae and

Barry Weinhold in their book, *The Flight from Intimacy: Healing Counter-Dependency*, put it,

> *Adults who use violence or abuse to try to control children usually experience a triggering event that causes them to reenact an unhealed developmental trauma that occurred in their own childhood.*[71]

To shaming and controlling, I want to be sure and include coercion and manipulation, which are equally toxic and injurious to children. The key here, is that when the adult is triggered, he or she ceases to make rational choices and, instead, reenacts (automatically, and mostly unconsciously) the abuse that was meted out to him or her as a youngster. "Aware parents," the Weinholds say, "learn to recognize when they are being triggered by their child's behavior, and work on themselves rather than getting upset with the child."[72] Doing the work does involve a number of steps, including getting the right kind of support, allowing ourselves to know what happened to us, learning to be compassionate and supportive of ourselves and learning to gradually unblock, feel, and release the feelings that we could not have allowed ourselves to feel.

While the behaviors of coercion and manipulation and shaming and controlling are all injurious to children, they fall into a category of abuse just short of their more obviously violent counterparts that tend to come to mind when one thinks of child abuse. There is yet another category of stressors, however, responsible for disorganized attachment that are "softer" yet, but apparently even more damaging. We will talk about them a little later, under the heading of Affective Errors. First we will talk about what Gabor Máte refers to as not what *happened (that was damaging)* but rather what *didn't* happen *and was critically needed.* These are things such as attachment, touch, attunement, resonant connection, relational dialog, being seen, consistency/predictability, unconditional love, permission to have needs, permission to say no, and healthy adult role models.

Attachment

> *Of all of the primary tasks of the infant, there is none more crucial than the pursuit, acquisition and establishment of joyful, securely attached relationships.*
>
> — *Allan Schore in The Soul of Shame*[73]

Secure attachment between parent and child fosters autonomy. A child who grows up securely bonded with at least one parent feels safe enough to venture out and explore the world. He knows he can return to the safety of the parent, and can venture out at his own pace and in his own time, as he learns how to navigate the world and his own capabilities. There are numerous windows of opportunity along the course of development for faulty bonding to be repaired. But the correct ingredients need to be present for such repairs. Some of the things that are necessary to foster a healthy bond during the child's first five years are as follows:

Touch

"Touch," it is said, "is trust in the form of a hand or kiss."[74] In modern Western culture, often in the midst of material abundance and informational hyper-availability, so many of us suffer from touch starvation. Our culture gives us way more red lights than green ones when we are navigating what is safe and appropriate and what is off limits or shameful with regard to touching not only other people, but also ourselves. If you grew up feeling a little funny about touch, it's probably at least partly because our (over-sexualized, over-commercialized, and ironically sexually repressed) culture gives us very mixed and confusing messages about touch.

Due to research, we now know that the mammalian brain requires physical touch in order to properly develop. Touch receptors in the skin respond to closeness, cuddling and touch by signaling the production and release of oxytocin, which reduces stress levels in the body. Less stress translates in the body as more safety, comfort, and security, the essential elements of trust that facilitate bonding, according to Richo.[75] Growth and development of the orbitofrontal cortex is also known to be directly influenced by interactions within a mother-child bond, especially through physical touch.[76] Suffice it to say, if touch is a trigger to unconscious, unresolved trauma for a parent, interruptions in attachment will show up with their children, who will have hurdles to overcome in the area of trust, pleasure and interpersonal relations. Alexander Lowen, in his groundbreaking book Bioenergetics, says:

> *A mother is an infant's first ground, or to put it differently, an infant is grounded through its mother's body. Earth and ground are symbolically identified with the mother, who is a representative of ground and home […] My patients failed to develop a sense of being grounded or rooted because of a lack of sufficient pleasurable contact with their mothers' bodies […] A mother who is herself uprooted cannot provide the sense of security and grounding a baby needs.[77]*

Attunement

Adequate attunement is crucial to the development of a socially healthy individual. The development of healthy boundaries, sense of self, emotion regulation and trust are all contingent on sufficient attunement and nurturing during the first months and years of a child's life. In my class, Boundaries 101,[78] I make the distinction between resonant connection and attunement in the context of what we can do as adults if we discover that our boundaries are yet unformed or in need of repair. For our current purposes, these two terms are closely related, but different enough to examine for their unique contributions to the subject, which we will do in a moment. First a little more on the broader term of attunement.

The role of attunement in a child's ability to feel safe and to successfully attach (and hence, develop), is described in the following passage from Chris Fraley's *A Brief Overview of Adult Attachment Theory and Research.*

> *Children respond to an emotionally absent adult in a particular way. They have a built-in system that regulates proximity to the attachment figure. This system is continually checking to see if the attachment figure is nearby, accessible, attentive. If the answer is no, they respond with anxiety. As such, they exhibit attachment behaviors such as visual searching, active following and vocal signaling. Threat is gauged with regard to caregiver's affective signals of availability (rather than degree of actual threat).[79]*

A parent, under the best of circumstances, is equipped with a full set of instincts, awareness, and ability to sense the state of his or her child, and respond to those needs in ways that will nurture that child into healthy adulthood. This basic quality of being with another (and, as we will also see, oneself) and adjust one's behavior so that it is congruent with the other (or oneself) can be summed up as attunement. These ideas will be further explored in the following sections on resonant connection and relational dialog.

Resonant Connection is that aspect of attunement (between parent and child) that consists of an in-the-moment presence that is not threatened or significantly diminished by distractions that could potentially include dissociation, addictive patterns, worry, economic oppression, fear, self-doubt, or physical, social or mental challenges the parent might be facing at any particular time that prevents him or her from being available to the child and his or her needs. In Chris Fraley's quote above, this is referred to as emotional availability.

Relational Dialog (or social engagement), as a component of attunement, is a two-way collaborative dialog that encompasses emotion, symbol, and what is mutually shared between parent and child. A comprehensive discussion of attunement needs to include the idea of social engagement. With the healthy parent, such back and forth relating happens effortlessly as a result of its inherent rewards. When this dialog is working well enough, according to Essex, et al.,

> [T]he parent elicits the child's contributions and actively considers his experience, and an expression of this consideration on the part of the parent is demonstrated back to the child in developmentally appropriate ways that will be understood by the child.[80]

"Social engagement provides the neural platform upon which attachment processes can occur," according to

Stephen Porges, research professor in the Department of Psychiatry at the University of North Carolina at Chapel Hill, Emeritus Professor of Psychiatry at the University of Illinois in Chicago, and creator of The Polyvagal Theory. "Signals of safety," he says, "are the preamble to attachment."[81] They provide the felt sense of safety the child needs in order to physiologically bond with the parent. He is talking here about subtle, mostly unconscious, nonverbal cues a healthy mother is sending to her child all the time, that tell the child that he or she is wanted, a priority, and safe.

The internalization of this back-and-forth interaction, or dialog, it is said, provides a sense of enduring safety and reliable comfort in times of distress, and serve as a foundation for healthy adult relationships. The tendency to dissociate, on the other hand, is strongly linked to a lack of or primary failure of this parent-infant dialog. When the dialog does not occur, or is interrupted and not repaired, the child can sense this as a profound loss, and even a threat to survival.

Dialog happens at both conversational and demonstrative levels. Where at the conversational level there is a literal conversation between the child and the adult caretaker, the demonstrative level expands to take in the parent's behavioral responses to the child's unique and changing needs.

So while resonant connection describes the quality of the connection, relational dialog, or social engagement, is that aspect of attuned relating that is age- and role-appropriately bi-directional. The infant's or child's capability to dialog changes as he or she develops, along a pretty standard course. The parent's part of the dialog involves verbal and nonverbal language, gesture, facial expressions, and demonstration of love, availability, care and protection. What is clearly the role of the adult is the ability to make adjustments in his or her responses to the child and to the environment based on the child's needs. Because developmental needs can be an area of such obscurity and confusion, I include Barry and Janae Weinhold's chart on developmental stages in Appendix IV.

Successful attunement with a child who is throwing a tantrum might require parental awareness about what is happening situationally, as well as developmentally for a child of this age, and then in a non-punishing, non-judgmental way, minimize damage by helping to remove breakable or dangerous objects in the vicinity of the child, allowing the child to have a cooling off period (without disconnecting emotionally), and later approaching the subject with acute listening and neutral curiosity, gauging the readiness of the child to re-visit what has happened, and supporting the child while he or she gains language and alternative coping strategies when facing overwhelming emotions.

A basic need in childhood that often falls through the cracks is support in dealing with emotions, which can come in the form of role modeling, preverbal communication, and dialog about emotions using words as the child gains the language to engage. David Richo says that the power to self regulate (self soothe and modulate emotions when stressed) comes from attunement, and that attunement has to do with the allowing of our feelings. In his book, *Daring to Trust*, he says:

> *When there was no such attuning to our feelings, we may be possessed by them or block them. We will find it difficult to stay with our feelings, to address, process, and resolve them.*
> [82]

Richo's words above also allude to the attuning to oneself in order to properly regulate emotions. What I find particularly fascinating here is the idea that the resonant connection and relational dialog that make up attunement that we are talking about here in the context of parenting, is actually the same thing as the adult ability to connect with his or her own sense of self, emotions, in-the-moment experiences and needs.

The parent's degree of consciousness (or, we might say, embodiment) will determine the success of the relational dialog. Whether the parent is able to engage in these levels of dialog in ways that match up with the child's needs (consciously and/or intuitively), or "just goes through the motions" in a state of dissociated shutdown or distraction, is always apparent to the child. The better the mental health of the adult, the more seamlessly he or she will be able to take cues from the child to make adjustments to his or her behavior and the environment to ensure a child's well-being and safety, foster appropriate growth and development and convey a sense of security, belonging and connection to the child.

Being Seen

I'm not sure there is more here that isn't included in the attunement section, above, but I have more words I want to add. Maybe what I'm about to say is actually the same thing as attunement, but what I'm wanting to elaborate on is the importance, as an infant and a small child, of both the parental seeing of me, complete with all my needs, and their action on my behalf so that, in my state of complete dependence, I feel confident that I have the support I need to survive, that my needs do not make me less loveable, and that they do not significantly trouble my parents. This, to me, feels like acceptance. Not approval, but unconditional acceptance of my whole embodied self. And it involves my experience of sensing my parents as they engage fully with their senses and their intuition in such a way that I learn who I am and what my needs actually are. Through this mirror of their reaction to me, my needs become valid, and I learn that they matter; that I have the support that I need on my life's journey of finding out what makes me unique, what my skills are, and what I came here to do. The moment of birth is an appropriate time to engage such exploration (prior to birth, the mother's biology automatically responds to the developing fetus' needs, and so there is immediate and automatic feedback and supply of developmental needs in utero). The need to be seen is a vital one, and being seen contributes to healthy attachment in ways that are subtle but profound.

Consistency, Predictability

Consistent responses by parents also foster secure attachment. There are many things that can stand in the way of consistency, including economic or relational stress, trauma, mental illness, chaos and addiction. When a parent is triggered, he shows a face that is very different from the one he wears when he is not triggered. Moreover, a child of a parent who is chronically or repeatedly depressed feels his parent's emotional absence even when she is physically present. In either of these situations, what the child tends to perceive is a sudden and/or unpredictable changeability, which he or she naturally attributes to some personal defect or something he or she (the child) has done to bring about the change. In the case of the latter (maternal depression), the parent uses a manufactured, fit-for-public façade when interfacing with people outside the family. All of the factors I list above, along with others I've inevitably overlooked, can be major motivators for an unhappy parent to present a mask of "normalcy" to the world when he or she is struggling and can't imagine receiving the kind of support that would make a difference.

Rage can be another cause of abrupt change in a parent's mood and body language. The infant's response to inconsistency from a parent during a time of heightened stress might range from feeling generally unsafe to a physiological terror response, to shutdown, and possibly the tendency to use dissociation as a coping mechanism. Unrepaired, the experiencing of a parent's changeability has been found to have a negative impact on attachment. We will explore this more in the section entitled Affective Errors.

Unconditional Love (Acceptance)

Children are engineered to seek the approval of their parents. And they instinctively respond to parental approval, as a signal of what it takes to gain acceptance, which children need like air and water. To this end, children begin at a very young age to internalize the "rules" of the household, which are taught and enforced largely through approval. These internalized rules are what they use to navigate childhood. It is important to distinguish, however, between approval (that is earned through doing the right things) and acceptance, which is unconditional. "I" was accepted with enthusiasm when I helped, agreed and complied. But there was no margin for me to venture out of this role. Therefore, it was not me that was accepted, but rather the role I assumed. And I felt some acceptance as long as I stayed within it. Venturing out, I was not so sure. Love, for me, did not reside in my heart, but rather my head. It was constantly calculated and elicited, consciously and unconsciously, through controlling behaviors. It did not feel warm, comfortable, or safe.

Permission to Have Needs

Because of the culture of my parents' unexamined wounds and beliefs, it did not feel appropriate or even safe to ask for anything. The price of asking was complicated, unspoken, confusing, and it felt dangerous, so I rarely risked it. My identity became *I don't make unnecessary demands on [their] resources or time.* What I later realized about this strategy is that it carried with it a second assumption: *It's not okay to have needs.* This was the strategy and the identity I carried into my adult relationships. As you may be able to guess by now, this was not a functional strategy for intimacy, or even lasting friendships. And I would need to develop a language around my needs and learn about boundaries before I could actually pull this all together into a working model for relating in healthy, authentic ways with others.

I grew up very confused about needs. Entering therapy for the first time at about age 25, my therapist mentioned unmet needs, and I began to try to sort out my needs from my wants. I thought of things like clothes, and things I might have asked my parents for if they'd had a little extra money—and nice, fancy things I could only imagine someone else being able to actually provide for me. At 25 I was floundering, having been raised to believe that I needed a man to manage the money side of life, but not having been able to pull that off for reasons I'm beginning to understand now. But then at a very practical level I knew that none of those things were unarguably *needed*. More likely they fell into the category of wants. So what were my needs, anyway? It took me a while to circle back to this question, probably as a result of the passage of some years, a degree in social work, and a couple jobs in the field. At just the right time, though, I met just the right person: Philomina Gwanfogbe Ph.D., Food, Nutrition, and Lifestyle Coach. I attended her lecture at a nearby health food store, and listened to what she had to say. A few things she said surprised me. One was that when we feel hungry, sometimes it's not food we're hungry for. She listed things we might check for before peering into the refrigerator or stopping by a fast-food joint, in case we were hungry for something besides food. Her list of *"primary foods"* that provide nourishment that we can't get from actual edibles include:[83]

• Special Relationships
• Nourishing Spiritual Practices
• Satisfying Work/Career
• Things we Love
• Loving Treatment of our Bodies

I had no idea that these were basic needs we all have as human beings. And like many others (I presume), I had been confusing the basic need for these things for hunger. When we confuse loneliness, emotional emptiness and general discontent with hunger, food doesn't satisfy us. For me, this list provided an excellent starting point to create my own "primary foods" list, which I called my "primary needs" list.

Each of us has the responsibility of identifying our own needs. We are also quite capable of working toward meeting these needs for ourselves, though sometimes we do need to enlist the help of others.

Permission to have needs as a child is a necessary prerequisite to secure, healthy attachment. Knowledge about what basic social and emotional needs are and that they are pretty much universal is something that somehow fails to enter our curriculum in today's learning institutions, and many of our parents have come to adulthood not understanding that their needs are real and an important part of caring for themselves as well as being effective parents. I hope to be part of the solution to this serious problem. As sad as it is, many of us have missed the ideal window of opportunity to securely attach to our parents. But now is *exactly* the right time for me, as an adult, to nurture secure, healthy attachment to myself.[84] There is not a moment to lose.

Permission to Say No

Saying no, protesting, or negotiating were strongly discouraged, if not punished, in my family when I was young. I believe that my protest function had already been destroyed even before I learned to speak. One of the most important ways in which this was done was through my parents' way of meeting my sister's strong will. In response to her curiosity, questions and self-expression, they took a consistently rigid and unrelenting tack of shaping her into the "proper" girl they wanted from the time she began to walk. (She skipped crawling and went straight to walking and reading.) I learned by watching them interact that protest was futile, and negotiation a battle not worth the spoils.

Modeling of Healthy Adult Interaction

In healthy-enough families, adults model tools for building healthy intimacy for their children; how to repair relationships, how to navigate the world of social interactions and emotions. When a child is born into a family where neither of the parents are emotionally available or equipped to attune to their social and emotional needs, it sometimes happens that another adult is available to fill in for this deficit. But as mentioned in the Consistency, Predictability section, above, people who suffer from depression and mental illness tend to avoid social situations. Therefore, parents who suffer from these problems tend to not only deprive themselves of connection and support from others, but they can also deny their children contact with other healthy adults. Such is the case with Mandy, in the scenario below.

Mandy is four. She sees her mother day after day in the doldrums of a seasonal depression, or possibly hung over from her evening prescription of Jack and Coke. Her mom doesn't

94

get dressed when she gets up in the morning. Nor does she bother to tend to her appearance when she emerges from her room for unpredictable periods of time. She is haggard. When Mandy looks into her eyes, she is not there. Mom goes through the motions of her household responsibilities, but is not motivated, or capable of connecting with her child, whose physical needs, for all practical purposes, appear to be met. But something Mandy isn't old enough to identify is missing.

Grandmother calls. Mom picks up the phone and her voice changes. "Yes, everything is fine. George took those old tires up to the Joneses. It was the darndest thing." She laughs. It's a laugh that Mandy has not heard in days. She looks up at her mother. This change in her mother is something that does not escape Mandy. She wonders what to attribute it to. Is it something she can elicit somehow? Surely, she thinks, it is something about her that has caused the glum mood. If she could just change her behavior, maybe. If she could somehow be good enough, maybe she could get her mother's love back. Maybe she could make her happy. Mandy scans her memory banks for possibilities: What could she do to reach that switch? To get the attention and connection she so desperately needed?

The fact of the matter is, the changeability of a parent's moods has virtually nothing to do with the child. A parent with unresolved emotional issues will dissociate in response to strong emotions or uncomfortable situations, but can come back when necessary with a monumental (though unsustainable) act of will. Ironically, he or she does this to

95

preserve the illusion to the outside world that everything is fine. As is common with the culture of depression or addiction, the family puts on a mask of normalcy when it interfaces with anyone outside the family, to ward off suspicions that anything is out of the ordinary. As a result, the child rarely has interactions with healthy, emotionally available adults, and thus misses out on opportunities to get what she needs to traverse the developmental stages of bonding, separation and beyond. As an adult, she carries a battery of unmet needs, replaying the scenario by engaging in relationships with one emotionally unavailable person after another.

When Caregivers are Overwhelmed

When caregivers are overwhelmed because of their own difficulties, they can inadvertently teach their children that the world is not a safe place, leading them to become fearful, frustrated, withdrawn or disorganized. In fact, ample research shows that there is a strong relationship between a caregiver's unresolved memories of trauma or loss leading to disorganized attachment in their children. Findings from a Princeton study of 14,000 children in the US in 2014[85] suggest that

> *[forty] percent lack strong emotional bonds—what psychologists call "secure attachment"—with their parents that are crucial to success later in life, according to a new report. The researchers found that these children are more likely to face educational and behavioral problems.*[86]

Research of Mary Main, attachment researcher at UC Berkley, indicates that probably more than 46 percent of the general population has a disorganized attachment style. In her research she also shares an astonishing figure that suggests that this figure is about 80 percent among mental health practitioners.[87]

It would only follow that parents—including middle-class parents—need more support to provide proper parenting, and that channeling resources accordingly would make a whole lot of sense for our country. Such support might include shifts in our culture to support the value and availability of high quality, affordable mental healthcare; family leave; affordable, high-quality childcare; home visits for new parents by social workers specifically educated in human development; and income supports for mothers of young children.

It astounds me how attachment deficits are so prevalent in the US today, given the resources at our disposal, the breadth and depth of research that has been done, and the iconic image of development and resourcefulness that the United States represents all over the world. Nonetheless, the fallout of insecure attachment and its companions, social and emotional illiteracy, are apparent everywhere we look. The following section will examine the fallout of insecure attachment.

The Fallout: Results of Lack of Secure Infant Attachment

Disorganized attachment is the flavor of insecure attachment that has been flagged for higher risk of dissociation as a coping mechanism through adulthood. The disorganized attachment style is one in which the child exhibits a confusing combination of approach-avoidance behaviors with his or her parent. By definition, this attachment style is one in which the child is both frightened by and dependent on the adult caregiver, which poses an extremely stressful, unsolvable paradox for the child. This child will avoid or resist the parent, even if the parent's gestures, in the moment, are friendly or conciliatory. By the time the child demonstrates symptoms of disorganized attachment, he or she is already not sure it's safe to trust.

Attachment is such a strong and fundamental drive in infants and small children, that when it doesn't progress along its intended course, the child experiences a tremendous loss. Lacking "being seen" in this loss and the emotions that result, the child remains alone with his experience. What has been lost here is of immeasurable importance. The loss then becomes multi-layered, and in order to mitigate it, the child effectively suppresses his need for contact and communion, lest they overwhelm him. He will not risk the feeling of such devastation in the future, and any drive for communion and contact is overridden by the need to protect against having to go through that *ever* again. This shutdown is actually a form of despair about finding what he needs in others. The fundamental knowing that one is protected and that comfort is available is impaired, and in its place there is a very different working model.

A pretty clear and predictable set of problems show up when attachment goes wrong. Divergence from healthy attachment can take on various flavors (avoidant, anxious, disorganized), but regardless of the flavor, problems with relationships are the result. Children who do not have secure attachment with their parents are more likely to have poorer language and poorer behavior before entering school. These performance measures reflect many things; a few of the more obvious we will touch on now.

Emotional Regulation is one of the most apparent casualties of insufficient attachment. Emotional regulation is the ability to manage emotions as they come up, and navigate them in a way that is conscious and emotionally intelligent. When an individual cannot emotionally regulate, it means that he or she will be frightened of feeling their emotions, especially the vulnerable ones, and will cope by blocking them, and by using distraction or addiction in attempts to avoid dealing with them. When we lack emotional regulation, we don't know how to stay with our feelings, to address, process, or resolve them.

It will also mean that despite our best efforts, our unprocessed emotions will slip out sideways and hurt people and damage our closest relationships, in behaviors we have already referred to as regressive. What this can look like is the tendency to lash out or act out our intense feelings with others—that is, when we can't effectively suppress them. By the time we reach adulthood, and we figure out countless ways to suppress and distract ourselves from our emotions, it can show up as the somatization of emotions that are actually never felt but rather worn in the body in the form of tense muscles, energy- and oxygen-deprived tissues, overworked organs and disease. I look back at the overwhelm I experienced when faced with stress in my elementary school years, and understand it, finally, as lack of emotional regulation; an overwhelm that hijacked my ability to think, self-advocate or soothe myself. And I had no idea what to do about it.

I can't help but wonder whether increases in school shootings, bullying, youth suicide, and compulsive use of screen time (whether it's internet browsing, video games, or television) are the natural consequences of insecure attachment.

Individuation The natural developmental progression for a child is first bonding, and then separation. If bonding does not happen, to provide the strong-enough foundation of attachment, healthy individuation will not be able to occur. This then becomes evident in problems with distinguishing self from others (interpersonal boundaries) and identifying feelings, and therefore in identifying personal limits and needs.

Development of Self When a person fails to develop a sense of self, what tends to be very difficult is the prospect of connecting or bonding with the self, which is necessary for self love, self attunement and self advocacy. From this place, it is very difficult to communicate with others about emotions, wants, needs and limits, which is essential to building trust and intimacy.

Embodiment The basic disconnect with our bodies that results from both the physiological response to trauma, along with a chronic avoidance of negative emotions, has the effect of depriving us of self-information or interoception, and results in the perpetuation of lack of self-attunement with regard to emotions, needs and limits.

Personal Power Controlling others is the compulsive substitute defense strategy for true autonomy that follows healthy individuation, and the spontaneous development of emotional regulation following healthy attachment. Controlling and manipulation then serves as the poor man's version of true personal power.

Comfort and Protection Strategies Without having achieved any degree of healthy individuation, generally lacking trust in others, and managing deficits in emotional regulation, a developing youth will not naturally find comfort or protection from other people. Vulnerable feelings are hidden from herself as well as others. With her pain disguised, she will take an independent approach to problem solving. Seeking comfort and protection from others will not be included among her repertoire of coping strategies.

Because of the early, unresolved loss, intimacy is a trigger, and the inability to relax in intimate relationships is the result. Because of the basic inability to be soothed or comforted by another, relationship is not naturally restorative or nurturing; the person lacks the ability to receive the comforting, even if the partner is willing to give it. Over-reliance on individualism is the result, with the façade of independence hiding feelings of vulnerability, shame, and inadequacy.

The conclusion that we make very early on is that there is no help for us when we are stressed, that basically, we are on our own. We have no active synapses between stress and strategies for seeking comfort or protection. We endure. We brace ourselves. We rely on the deadening function that comes with hypoarousal. Until our bodies tell us they can't anymore. And then we are forced to begin to develop new strategies.

Healthy Intimacy And finally, those individuals who do not have secure attachment as infants tend to repeat these patterns with their intimate partners as adults. There are studies that suggest a modest overlap between how secure people feel with their mothers and their romantic partners. Among the research findings on this relationship is one from Chris Fraley's article,

> *Hazan and Shaver (1987) found that adults who were secure in their romantic relationships were more likely to recall their childhood relationships with parents as being affectionate, caring, and accepting.*[88]

Moreover, being part of a culture that tells us that we live happily ever after only when we find the mate of our dreams, yet experiencing time and again the pain and confusion of intimacy as a dissociative trigger, it is likely that those of us with insecure attachment will begin to confuse pleasure with pain. For us, happiness and heartache come packaged together.

INFANTS EXPERIENCE SHOCK WHEN SEPARATED FROM A PRIMARY CARETAKER.

(Infant Terror and Rage)

I guess it's safe to say, looking back at the patterns of my relationships, that I was not a securely attached child. With regard to attachment during my infancy and early childhood, I search the archives, and come up with something that happened. The words for this *happening* began to come to me when I was in my forties.

I'm second-born to a family of nine. By the time I was 4, my mother was giving birth again. That probably wouldn't have been so bad if it hadn't been for the fact that it happened again when I was 6, 7 and 8. By the time it happened again at 14, 16 and 18, it was just how life was.

It's taken some considerable research for me to understand the emotional impact all this had on me. My mother told me that for my birth, the gas they gave her made her very sick. As was standard procedure at the time, I was quickly shuffled away to the nursery, so she could recover during my first hours. She said that the effects of the gas would make her sick for weeks.

So for me, childbirth triggered one crisis after another not just because it reignited memories of my medicated, unattached birth, but also because my mother had a negative Rh factor, which made subsequent pregnancies a life-or-death ordeal. I have no doubt that my three-year-old ears picked up snippets of what the adults were talking about around me. I heard with child #3 that Mom shouldn't have any more children. It was too dangerous, her doctor had warned her. She could die, or the baby might die. One of my only memories of young childhood was deciding to run away. I might have been 7-8-9 (it's all kind of a blur, actually) because I could not see an end to the continuous stream of diapers, training pants and socks that I was tasked to hanging on the line. By the time I was 9 or 10 I fantasized a lot about leaving and taking care of myself in the woods. I practiced by building houses and imagining doing it all without support from anyone. I didn't want to be a burden, but I felt hopeless that I would ever be able to do anything besides somebody else's work. I doubt that was really the case. But it was a feeling I remembered having. Alone.

Of course I knew I could trust my mother, and her life was about selflessness, about fearlessly following the guidance she felt was available to her from her higher power. I knew that as long as she had health and life, she would work together with my dad to make sure we were provided for. But her lifestyle—one crisis after another—where I felt I could lose her literally and in fact I did emotionally, did not foster a feeling of safety or a feeling that there was room for me to have needs of my own. And all around me was evidence that there was not attention and care enough for me. Rather it was one cycle after another where Mom would have to go away and then when she came back she had another baby—more responsibility, and even less bandwidth left for herself or for me.

I was not so articulate—my words came late and slow, so I distracted myself from my fear, anxiety, grief, anger, by staying busy with caretaking and compliance. I could not face the feelings—so intense, or articulate my fears and expect to be heard. What were my little fears in the face of her mortality, the crisis of the day? And I would assume the role of caretaker because that was the road that opened up before me. Being what people needed me to be—until the crisis passed. But it never really felt like the crisis had an endpoint. Life was one crisis swell followed by the next. Relationship was doing to avoid catastrophe and discomfort, whether it was keeping my mother alive by managing my siblings so that as a unit we were less of a burden, or by helping prop up her fragile self-esteem by essentially merging with her and helping her maintain at least an image of a "normal" family. Relating was the satisfaction I could get when I successfully anticipated the needs of others—particularly hers.

Affective Errors

This statistic, cited in a Princeton study in 2014, particularly struck a chord with me:

> One study showed that among a group of children who lacked secure attachment, demonstrated by an avoidance or resistance of their parents (40% of the overall group), 25 percent avoided their parents because their parents were ignoring their needs, and 15 percent were resisting their parents because their parents were causing them distress.[89]

These mothers, being watched by researchers, were apparently unaware of the damaging nature of their behaviors, which is no surprise. They were triggered (like the parents at Wal-Mart). And besides, they were treating their children exactly the way they had been treated by their parents.

While I did not think or "know" that my parents were causing me distress or ignoring my needs, this was what my body experienced and it reacted accordingly. This bodily memory set into motion a lifetime of physical constriction and relationships that felt similarly unsafe and confusing, and which validated my experience that it was not safe to trust.

Things can go wrong between a child and her parents that don't constitute abuse, but nonetheless result in degrees of disorganized attachment and the propensity toward dissociation and problems with relationships later in life. These "quieter" caregiving deviations are referred to in the literature in a number of ways, including hidden trauma, and disruptions in maternal affective communication. Maybe a broader way of looking at this set of parental behaviors is by classifying them as affective errors. They result in confusion and abandonment because the adult is not properly understanding the child or his or her needs.

The behaviors, though not explicitly hostile or intrusive, interrupt normal bonding processes so that the child does not feel safe and prepared for subsequent developmental milestones. The kinds of parental behaviors we are talking about include chronic non-responses, contradictory responses, role-reversed responses, withdrawal from emotional contact, frightened or frightening responses and disoriented responses. They are especially damaging when the adult responds with these behaviors in response to the child when the child is upset and in need of comforting.[90]

Chapter 4 - Bringing the Body into the Conversation

The body actually has plenty to say about all this trauma, dissociation and the brain, and it does, all the time, in countless ways. In what ways do we listen? Our bodies actually talk to us continuously, using the primitive language they share with nature and dreams. This information is readily available to us not in words, but nevertheless through metaphor, through aches and pains, tension, moisture, trembles, grumbles, strength and weakness, color, texture, temperature, sensation...the list goes on and on. Let's just imagine for a moment what the body might say if it could talk to us in words; it seems to me that it would be succinct and to the point.

- *You need not be afraid of me.* At some level, you may see your body as a spoiled, childlike tyrant, and if you do, it would make sense that you would be afraid to listen to it. *Give it an inch and it might take over completely, right?* But don't be confused. *That* is your ego you're thinking of. Your body has never been the enemy. Your body has actually been there for you this entire time, through thick and thin, abuse, neglect, abandonment—all of it. Your body (pardon the pun) has your back. In fact, your body may even be the very wisest and most loyal part of you.

- *There are some things I need you to know about me. First of all, when you get stressed and when you disconnect from me, I naturally tighten up in order to protect you.* When you are triggered, here's what the body does: clamp down, draw in, constrict. I wasn't paying attention before, but now that I am, I can see how true this is.

- *When you ignore me, you ignore and cut off vital parts of yourself at your own peril.*

- *When you were small, and you were afraid, or felt unsupported, I came to your aid by providing you with ways to get the help you needed, through the tone and quality of your voice, your facial expressions, your muscle tone. I am why you cried and wiggled so.* As we have already learned, not having developmental needs met results in chronic levels of physiological arousal. What might have appeared to your family as bad behavior or a temper tantrum was not calculated or manipulative on your part. It was your body's normal response to stress, and you had not developed any measure of self-regulation yet, which infants are reliant on their adults to help them with. And if your family just kept ignoring you, or punished you for being upset, you would naturally adapt, developing strategies to better utilize your energy. In a way, this is when you learned that asking for what you wanted from others was not going to get you what you needed. And it may have been the very first point of dissociation—between what was happening inside and what was happening outside of you. After all, if you were rewarded for "good behavior" and being good for your parents meant being quiet, you would naturally do what you could to gain their approval and acceptance and avoid being a burden to them by keeping quiet.

- *I can communicate in much more sophisticated ways than you ever knew.* You know about up and down. You know about left and right. You know about weak and strong. But take a moment and consider the fact that these are pretty arbitrary mental constructs—points on the extreme ends of duality *spectrums*. Your body, if you will attune to it, can speak to you in much subtler language that involves all the gradations of reality in-between the extremes and so much more besides. Yes. Your 3-D body is willing and able to do this for you. The body is an ingenious, highly calibrated instrument. Subtleties are its syntax. As we get to know our bodies, we learn that we have pain and pleasure, and all the stations in between. And healing from trauma involves becoming aware of these nuances. In order to recover from trauma, you will need to learn about nuance.

- *That pain you're feeling? It's repressed emotion.* Habitual stress-induced restriction in your muscles, joints and tissues tells the story of repressed emotions and trauma you carry around in your body. Such information is always available, giving us access to material that we need in order to move forward in our recovery. We talked about energy cysts in Chapter 1. These are body memories stored away in our muscles and tissues that we were not able to adequately process when overwhelming things happened to us so long ago. When we bring compassionate awareness to the contents of our energy cysts, they naturally resolve as the emotional debris from the past is released from our muscles and tissues, and we can finally relax and heal. Of course it's not simple, or you would have already done it long ago.

That's why you may need some help in dealing with them. You may also need a little support and education before you know how to provide them with the care they require. There is no shame in this. And the work is completely doable. Pain is simply the body's way of getting your attention. The wisdom of the body created the energy cyst to protect you during a time when adequate resources were not available to you. But you are older now, and have access to so much more. Besides, it takes energy to keep that information locked inside. Now your energy is needed elsewhere, and your cysts have become leaky, allowing that old pain to enter into your awareness. Information from tight muscles, achy joints and energy cysts can help us reconstruct (and tell) the story. They can also tell us when it is time for change, in our relationships with ourselves and others. So get ready. Change is good.

- **You have treated me as so much unwanted baggage.** If you want to be really honest, you know it's true. You've blamed your body in so many ways. People, especially people who are habitually disconnected from their bodies, view the body as something they have to carry around with them, a number on a scale, the thing that keeps them from being happy, the thing that makes them different. But know this: your body has been placed in your care, it is under your direction. It does what you command it to do through repeated thoughts, your actions, your attitudes, beliefs, and expectations of it (conscious or not).

- **I am the outward manifestation of your thoughts and beliefs.** Got some work to do? That's okay.

- **You've been so busy; you don't think you have the time to tune in to what I need. But that couldn't be further from the truth.** Is your lifestyle appropriate and sustainable to your health? Do you even have time to think about this? Unfortunately, the time needed to do this is not going to just present itself to you. You have to reach out and claim it. No one is going to do this for you. And it's such an important thing that only you can do. You are important enough. Those other things can certainly wait. What needs to change in order for you to be happy and healthy, mind and body?

- *I am the one thing that anchors you in the present moment. Not yesterday. Not tomorrow. I am Now.*

- *Pain has been the only way you'll listen to me.* Once you take an interest in what your body has to say, and begin to understand nuance, it will not need to be difficult. The dialogue between you and your body will become a natural part of your keenly intelligent, highly attuned navigational system.

- *When you flee from the discomfort of emotions, you are abandoning me.* Avoiding emotions is one way we unwittingly abandon ourselves.

- *Feeling abandoned by the most important people in your life? That's how I feel.*

- *The way you treat me? That's how you were treated.* It's time to tell the story. Once it is really told, and you can listen to it with compassion, you will be able to forgive all the characters in the story and move on.

- *You. Don't. Even. Know. Me.* I have gone through my life without really knowing my body, much less befriending it. I've taken it for granted, I've blamed it, I've blocked emotions, I've done the bare minimum to keep it functioning. Now faced with the new awareness of physical pain that can come with age when we've been chronically disconnected, I realize that I am at a crossroads: I can continue to escape the pain, or I can attune to my body and allow it to guide me, to teach me about what it needs.

- *I've been operating in Crisis Mode for so, so long. I need your help to switch over to the Rest and Recuperate Channel. Please.* Trauma, as we discussed in Chapter 1, is what happens when the body does not recover from crisis. The body didn't get the memo that the frightening, unacceptable ordeal is finally over. It therefore believes it is *still* in crisis. Until the body recovers, the crisis isn't over. In crisis mode, besides having the effect of keeping you from being able to discern the past from the present, your bodily senses remain blunted, so you're not especially aware of what's happening physiologically (these chemicals, remember, are what make it possible for us to fight or escape and survive in times of real danger).

- *In Crisis Mode, I'm running a program that tells your brain that you're in danger. That's how I'm designed.* The stress response stays alive even after the stressful situation has passed. Therefore, information from the tense, constricted body sends information to the brain telling it that you are still not safe. The cascade of cortisol and adrenaline continues to flow through your system, readying muscles, interrupting digestion, increasing vigilance, increasing heart rate. And the cycle continues.

- *I have been doing my best to get your attention because I'm stuck here, and it's frankly exhausting. I have no idea how to change this channel, but I can't keep going like this.* When the overwhelm of trauma happens, and the body responds by switching into fight or flight (Crisis Mode), it naturally needs help switching back into rest and recuperate mode (parasympathetic nervous system/PNS). Stuck in sympathetic response, it is scanning the environment and providing you with information to keep you safe from danger, even when no real danger exists in the here and now.

- **Soothing comfort and pleasure are important ways you can help me switch to PNS.** Remember Karla McLaren's theory of trauma and the three stages of initiation? Remember that crucial third stage that is so essential to recovery: being welcomed unconditionally by the tribe, being seen, being physically held and cared for. And even having our wounds cleaned, treated and bound. Receiving these things from others can engender a felt sense of safety, connection, body rejuvenation, recovery and resolution. But receiving them from *yourself* works just as well, sometimes even better. Be compassionate with yourself as you begin to learn this new language. The best way to start is by experimenting with what feels good and right to you. Allow yourself time to learn. Be patient but persistent as you learn. Go slowly. This may be completely new and uncharted territory for you.

- **I can actually be calmed and quieted the same way babies and animals can be calmed and quieted.** Your body is actually acting no different than a frightened animal. You can quiet it by holding and touching it, by being very much in tune with it, by going slow. By protecting it, feeding it and rocking it, and by very gradually exposing it to new things as appropriate.

- **Attune to me the way you would have wanted to be attuned to.** Attachment during childhood is what enables and fosters sense of self, boundaries, and trust. It is completely within your ability *now* to afford your body the care, attention, and attunement it needs to foster an adult sense of self, adult boundaries and adult trust. You've been so interested in the feelings of others. Now it's time to shift that focus to yourself.

- *I've been all constricted (for nothing) and I need oxygen and circulation to maintain the health and vigor you expect from me.* Gentle, intuitive exercise such as tai chi or yoga under the instruction of a skilled coach or teacher is a good place to start. They are both excellent ways to care physically for your body, expand your awareness of it, and increase your ability to live in the present moment.

- *You've been giving me orders I wasn't designed to carry out. Expecting me to look sexy (whatever that means), or work long hours without adequate care or appropriate rest or nutrition are ways you abuse us both. Stop it.*

- *Attune to me, and my needs. When my needs are met, we both win.* When you make use of the body's wisdom, you move through the world and your relationships more fully informed. Being in partnership with your body is a win-win proposition. Your body gives you a continuous stream of valuable signals—if you can learn to read them, you'll understand when you need to say no, take time out, pause, reboot, regroup, and connect with yourself and know what is truly important to you.

- *Take time to be still and listen. I'll tell you what I need.* Effective recovery from trauma must involve the body, mindfulness and the senses. You are the only one who can turn this cycle around.

CHILDHOOD ABANDONMENT & SEXUAL ABUSE

"It's like, do I bond or do I survive?"

I watched Lu, over the brief months of our work together, respond to her body's invitation for intimacy, and gain a greater understanding of the tangible benefits of listening to what it was telling her. What she is also learning is that for it to be okay to be in her body, she needs tools.

Lu's story might be told beginning at her birth, when her mother was very, very, very sick. It's a tangled path from these beginnings to her adult penchant for uncertainty to committing in relationship, fear of being separated, and history of turbulence and intensity in intimate relationships. Lu struggles, but finally finds the words to describe the confusing feeling from very early in life: "It's like," she says, *do I bond or do I survive?"*

Lu's mother left the home when Lu was only three. And as if that weren't enough, Lu experienced several years of sexual abuse that started shortly after her mother left. At six, she finally decided to tell someone. Unfortunately, although the abuse stopped, she was not believed, and the people in her family who had been involved were angry with her for telling.

Prior to deciding to work with a psychotherapist, Lu received bodywork from a massage therapist for a year, targeting, among other things, sensations she had in her neck. In the process of doing this therapy, memories would invariably surface. The masseuse would press. Lu would have to let go. Lu persisted through the many, many tears that came from this important bodywork. So many, in fact, that she believed there was nothing left. It was in her work with me that she accessed the remaining layers, and that she learned she could send her vulnerable inner six-year-old to her safe grandmother's house in her imagination when we went on to address that material. With her inner six-year-old safely at her grandmother's, the adult Lu could deal with the adult issues that still needed her attention.

> Grandmother's House: My eyes are closed. She is rubbing my legs. Behind her house there is a big valley, a meadow, a creek, and a hill full of trees. That's where we go. At Grandmother's House, I can imagine; I can be anything I want to be.

Lu says that sometimes her body seems to know things that her mind doesn't, usually related to trauma. Over the past several years she has noticed that there are patterns to how her body feels, related to the time of the year that something traumatic happened in her life that she has not clearly processed or allowed her body to fully feel and heal from. So we utilize body sensations that show up in session to direct our attention and work.

In one of our sessions together, we addressed a pain Lu had in her head. The event that triggered this pain was a physical battering she had received at the hands of her current partner when he had been in an unconscious blackout, which is something that would happen to him anytime he had more than four alcoholic drinks. This Lu had known; but they were working on it.

As we targeted the pain in Lu's head, she noticed it move gradually to the left. Taking up about a quarter of her head at first, it began to get smaller. During this session, the pain transformed into total forgiveness that Lu didn't understand, but could palpably feel. From it emerged a knowing that she would need to set some important boundaries. The abuse and the bruises that resulted also helped Lu connect with a memory about another time when she had experienced a similar feeling. It had been six years earlier, on her way to the chiropractor. She had been in an unloving relationship with her daughter's father. She recalled the splitting right temporal lobe, attributing the feeling to being "too intense."

The relationship this incident brought to mind had been deeply painful. But through the use of imagery, body-directed therapy, attunement and bilateral stimulation, Lu has been able to apply this new understanding about her need for boundaries to all her adult relationships. It also helps her to feel empowered in the co-parenting of her daughter, who has special sensory-related needs.

Lu's daughter, not unlike Lu's body (and in a similar language), demands her attention, often in ways that cannot be ignored. In her words:

> Being a mom is difficult for me. I'm flying by the seat of my pants. We're both children in a way. I want to learn how not to be a child. In this house, it's war at times.

Nowadays, Lu believes her young daughter to be a very important teacher. What she learns from her is to let go; to not be so intense. "I played Legos with her," Lu tells me. "I usually resist. But I was very present with her, and my body felt heavy (grounded). She wants me to play her way. She tells me, '*Mom, you just build things*.' She brings me back to the physical: *girl, surf board, jeep*." To explain the bruises she had received at the hands of her partner, Lu told her daughter she had run into a door, but it would take more than flimsy stories and makeup to conceal the tension and pain she was hiding.

Lu recalls a time when her parents were fighting and arguing just prior to her mother's leaving when Lu was three. "I could no longer feel connected to them," Lu said. "I was in a body and separate (from them) for the first time. I was scared. I got out of bed. I have a vivid memory of this moment. Dad was on the couch. Mom was standing at the stove. I walked down the hall, saw them there and asked, 'How come I can only feel myself?'"

It was an incredibly sad and lonely feeling, and one not easily put into words. That's why it is only now that she has finally found them. What had propelled her out of bed so long ago was confusion, and the feeling/belief: *I can't feel them and be okay (at the same time)*. At three years of age, she necessarily had to disconnect from her parents; it was too painful to stay connected.

Lu is a camper, a gardener. She does these things to help her stay connected to the earth, to stay grounded. In the wintertime, when it's not so easy to stay connected, she quilts. The colors and textures help her stay in her body. "I've been in this unattached/ungrounded mode for a long time," she says. In our sessions and our processes together, I capture what she says. It comes forth like a poem—the voice of her body-child reaching for contact.

Grounding

I can feel when my body is starting to lift.

I have to talk to it like a child.

Today I found–

lying on my back in the living room

pushing through sorrow

Talking to myself–

What do I want?

To forgive others.

I don't want any of those things stuck.

I want to be love,

and to forgive myself when I'm not.

I am getting stronger every day.

I have a body, I have a lot of things to do with it.

For as long as she can remember, Lu has been able to feel conflict remotely from people she cares most about. She tends to feel it in her neck. When they are experiencing conflict, she can feel it. She is currently learning how to separate what's hers and what's not. Her body has helped her understand that the habit of feeling the emotions of others is not healthy for her. Toward the end of our work together, she would get a nosebleed anytime she began thinking about what she calls "doing someone else's (emotional) work."

The guilt.

It's not mine.

It's delicate.

Noticing, releasing.

They used to be painful.

Now more subtle.

I grieved for my younger self.

Grief—Deep sorrow for a sense of HOME.

I would have never thought of it as a gift.

I'm learning to love myself.

I can sleep a little better.

Experiencing glimpses of my own joy.

Shifting her awareness from the emotions of others to her own inner experience enables her own healing process to engage. Being in her own body is essential to this work, and it offers up bits of memory in the form of bodily sensations that we continue to pursue, examine, and then release.

I've been in this unattached/ungrounded mode

for a long time.

To the little body it feels like uncertainty.

Infant Lu.

Flailing limbs.

Uncomfortable, small,

can't feel my body.

Not knowing.

Not understanding.

Need to put light to it.

Light

Very strong root.

Need to plant a root.

I need to root.

But

Roots make me feel like I'm cutting off

separating

(staying)

I don't want to stay.

Uncertainty to committing.

Afraid of being separated.

Do I bond or do I survive?

Intellectually, Lu understood that the very tactile activity of gardening connected her with herself, but she sensed danger in sending down roots; in committing. There was a lingering ambiguity, fear about committing that we had not yet successfully addressed. Working with her body's wisdom, we came to transform that fear.

The light was still with me.

But now

it's not outside me. It's rather

behind me.

Operating me. Like I'm not cut off….

There's an openness

in my back

(behind me)

....It's flowing

not separate.

My mind didn't know,

but my body did.

I'm loved from beyond.

I matter.

It all matters.

In synthesizing her experience at the end of our work together, she shared with me a new understanding she had of herself. Everything suddenly made sense—the importance of the boundaries she had begun to set. Learning about boundaries, and beginning to set them, were steps that had to occur for the roots to go down. For it to be safe to connect. These boundaries had to do with separating her feelings and emotions from the feelings and emotions of others, and deciding to focus her attention on her own physical and emotional experience instead of the physical and emotional experience of others. And it also had to do with not allowing herself to be abused by others. These boundaries emerged and developed in the process of therapy, in the process of finding the words, and the process of allowing her emotions into her awareness.

ALL IS CONNECTED.

The Universe needs me to be me.

My tendency to move into the confusion of others

is both a gift and a curse.

There's a world I haven't expressed.

THERE IS NO FINISH LINE.

If there's no race,

there's no need to finish first.

Just a path, a place

I'm in it.

THIS IS IT.

Now I can root.

My body understands.

Awareness

There's still

(body tensing)

Fear of lack

Not ready to go.

It's so curled up.

I'm honoring it.

Spiral of blue and dark.

My energy field.

Compressed Ripped/Pulled

Like on an airplane.

Something there where it was.

Same image but in negative.

It's superimposed.

It felt that I loved it.

There's room now.

Where I didn't have room before.

That piece of me

That little slot

Now I get a chance to put something in there.

Re-name

Re-fill it.

With the beautiful trust I get.

I knew Saturday

that I feel whole.

From the deepest, wisest part of me

I hear

THERE IS NO FINISH LINE.

There's no need to finish first.

Body-Owner's Guide

Wiring

If listening to the perspective of the body is difficult for you, I can explain a lot of it in a much more left-brained way. There are very basic and logical reasons why we disconnect from our bodies under certain circumstances, and why reconnecting is necessary, possible, and just good common sense. If you take the time to do it, I'm convinced that you will never turn back. Before I offer my lists, I'd first like to tell you a little more about how our bodies are wired. As you may remember hearing, the automatic part of our nervous system (*the part that we have only indirect control over*) is the autonomic nervous system (ANS), which is made up of the sympathetic nervous system (SNS) and the parasympathetic nervous system (PNS).

The sympathetic nervous system (SNS) is responsible for helping the body prepare for emergency action (fight response and flight response), and for helping the body tolerate exercise. More specifically, it increases heartrate, inhibits digestion and salivation, dilates the pupils, relaxes bronchioles, stimulates liberation of glucose by the liver, signals the secretion of adrenaline and norepinephrine by the kidneys, relaxes the bladder, and contracts the rectum. It also helps blood flow and makes us feel alert and confident. According to Peter Levine, it "supports overall energy mobilization. If you are physically cold, perceive threat, or are sexually aroused, the sympathetic nervous system increases the metabolic rate and prepares you for action." And besides all that, it can, as it deems appropriate, signal reductions in the functions of the parasympathetic nervous system.

The parasympathetic nervous system (PNS) is responsible for activities of rest and recuperation. These include digestion, stimulation of saliva and gallbladder function, gestation, nurturance, restitution of tissue and cellular function, reduction of the heart rate, contraction of the pupils, bronchioles and bladder and relaxation of the rectum. According to Schore,[91] PNS activation promotes passive coping strategies such as withdrawal or disengagement, dissociation, and the immobility response.[92] Examples of passive coping styles include physical or emotional withdrawal. Emotions commonly associated with PNS function have a negative valence, such as shame, disgust, hopelessness, and despair.

But major discoveries are being made about the way the body is wired, and what we are learning about the role of the vagus nerve is changing everything. The vagus is the major nerve of the parasympathetic nervous system, which basically connects the brain to the body. It comes off the brain and "wanders" throughout the body. Its purpose is to connect the many different organs, including the throat, larynx, heart, lungs and gut, regulating body functions and sending information about their status back up to the brain.

Instead of having two branches of the autonomic nervous system, we actually have three. All three increase our chances of survival. The most recently developed branch of the vagus nerve, the ventral vagus, is responsible for social engagement. Next up is the sympathetic nervous system (SNS). And finally, the oldest of the three is the dorsal vagus, which acts very differently, depending on the organism's perception of safety. In times of life threat, the dorsal vagus takes over the newer systems and shuts down non-critical body functions, sometimes to immobilize us, and sometimes to allow us to blend in, and avoid being a target. Both help us to ensure survival. When it can, the body uses the newer systems to down-regulate the older systems. But if our system senses that fighting or fleeing are futile, the older dorsal vagus trumps everything to immobilize us.

When everything is functioning properly, we use our newest circuits first. When they don't serve to put us into safe environments, we move to older and more primitive circuits. The newest system, the ventral vagus or the social engagement system, is so called because it is in charge of the muscles of the upper face, the ears, and the vocal chords. As creatures designed to be dependent on our fellows for survival, our neuroceptors are particularly interested in information available here. And in a fraction of a second, dozens of interactions can take place below the level of awareness that give you a feeling about the person you are dealing with and determine how you will respond. It is through these means, they say, that big problems can be averted, by the subtle preconscious "negotiation" that takes place between two people, face to face.

Stephen Porges coined the term neuroception, which is the "body's ability to detect risk outside the realm of awareness."[93] Through neuroception, our nervous system is gathering information from the environment, and interpreting it below our awareness. This system is responsible for quickly shifting us into the states that are most likely to support our survival.

Breaking it down, many of the things that are picked up with neuroception can also be picked up with the conscious mind, if one is sensitive and informed. One can discern a lot about the emotional state of other people by paying attention to prosody, or the up-and-down, melodious aspect to the voice that cannot occur when someone is nervous; facial expressivity (whether there is animation in the upper part of the face, or it is flat); mood and affect; posture during social engagement; and muscle tension in the face (particularly around the eyes).

For those of us for whom bonding has been an enigma, it's not that we can't socially engage. It's more the case that social engagement (intimacy in particular, but also certain group settings) can require a lot of energy when, in fact, our species is uniquely built to use social engagement as a vital regenerative resource. As mammals, social engagement has the potential for helping us self-regulate, calm down, and recharge.

While dissociation, shock, immobility, sleep disorder, depression and catatonia are all dorsal vagal shut-down responses to stress, the vital functions of a well-balanced parasympathetic nervous system include rest and rebuilding, metabolism, healthy sleep, sexual arousal, and meditative states. The vagus nerve is the superhighway between the brain and the major organs and systems of the body, and researchers have spent entire careers trying to understand how it works. This sketch offers only a glimpse of our working knowledge of a highly complex system, but hopefully helps you to know at least a little bit more about how to effectively care for your equipment.

It's interesting to look back over my life and to observe what felt at the time like the failing of my own system under certain circumstances. When I have been scared or challenged, my expression goes flat and my voice goes monotone. And then there are certain circumstances where I am practically a different person, with more animation in face and voice. These times, I now understand, is when I have been able to let down my defenses. What has concerned me is my changeability, and sometimes the way I am just as suddenly disconnected from my own strength and resources. I am beginning to understand that this is a function of the autonomic nervous system, and that there is plenty I can do about it.

The way all this ideally works is that the sympathetic nervous system is modulated and regulated by the parasympathetic nervous system. And there is a nice, fluid flow back and forth to accommodate safety and optimal social interaction. But when the system has learned, very early on, that social engagement is not safe, as is the case with insecure and disorganized attachment, the body relies on its tried-and-true strategy: vigilance, which is a function of the SNS. One of the jobs of the sympathetic nervous system in times of great stress is to divert energy and resources away from the parasympathetic rest and restorative function. It can also have a less profound shutdown effect on the newer ventral vagus, affecting prosody in the voice, facial expressiveness, and listening ability, and use it for the more immediate issue at hand: survival.

What may also be happening with such attachment-challenged individuals is a system-wide parasympathetic dominance, which is responsible for energy conservation and offering the cloak of invisibility that can sometimes be our saving grace.[94] What we need to learn how to do is engage the healthy functions of the normal parasympathetic nervous system. I will offer a list of things that naturally do this later on.

Perhaps tongue-in-cheek, Porges says that we pay a big price for using the social engagement system, and that this "price" is our vigilance. I have two very separate responses to this statement. The first is from that of the individual who has experienced life through the lens of intimacy disorder. The other is from the perspective of recovery. As an insecurely attached person when I have been in intimate relationships, the price has always been too big. I did not want to give up the sense of control I had when I held fast to the safest thing I knew, which was vigilance and defensiveness. And until now I had no idea that I even had a choice in the matter. In fact, the price tag for not being able to reliably engage the social engagement system is failed adult intimacy. As a trauma therapist, and as a mother, a sister, and increasingly as a friend, I have experienced what it is to be enlivened by relationship, to relax, to allow myself to be seen, and to play. Porges says play is about mobilization (as opposed to immobilization), without our defenses, in a face-to-face setting.

It is so interesting to me that two people can have interactions that look virtually the same to the untrained eye, but the interactions make use of two very different systems: 1) hypervigilance to danger as supported by the SNS, though the hypervigilance can be largely indiscernible because of the habitual mask that has been created to send a convincing message that all is calm inside and 2) spontaneous and energizing prosocial engagement as supported by the ventral vagal system. These two systems, however, cannot both be active at the same time. We will talk more about hypervigilance in the next section.

What Porges is saying is that learning how to calm the vagus nerve is even more worthwhile than we may have imagined. He says that in turning off defensiveness we might not have even been aware of, we open ourselves to a whole new experience where interaction with others calms us, when it didn't before. When the upper face is animated, he says, vagal activity to the heart actually has a calming effect for the whole body. As Porges notes, this is the biological quest for "safety" in the proximity of another. It is what our nervous systems are looking for: safe places in a complex world. This is when we can be with others without our defenses. This is trust. From here arises the physiological phenomenon of attachment and bonding, from which emerges the possibility of two things: 1) the ability to be mobile, to be boldly, vocally and creatively ourselves and 2) the ability to feel so safe in relationship that we can allow ourselves to be immobilized without defensiveness.

Hypervigilance is one of the features of the sympathetic stress response. For people who as children were not sufficiently attuned to, hypervigilance is a common, chronic defensive response. The child learned to shut down his feelings because he didn't feel completely safe. He learned to be who others wanted and needed him to be because it was not safe actually being who he was. He spent a great deal of energy suppressing the warning responses his body generated, and with considerable expenditure of mostly unconscious energy he created an outward façade that communicated that he was "just fine." Regardless of this outer façade, his body remained on high alert, and he ceaselessly monitored everything going on around him for the sake of survival and safety. According to Allan Schore,

> Children develop ways to mitigate their attachment-related angst in relationships based on their attachment style. When separated and then reunited with their parents, insecurely attached children appear cool and unaffected. Some withdraw from their parents, and others approach their parents with ambivalence and resistance. Despite elevated heart rate and stress hormone levels, they appear to be minimizing attachment-related feelings and behavior (Ainsworth, 1971, 1978). They actually learn to disconnect (or dissociate) what is happening on the inside and what is happening on the outside.[95]

Whether or not he is in the presence of actual danger, his body is still highly activated, so he shuts down any potential to attend to feelings of loss or injustice or even personal preference. These don't serve him in this state of crisis. Instead of feeling himself, he feels the emotions of others. He is acutely sensitive

130

to the emotions of the people around him. Here is how Walker describes it:

> As a traumatized child, your over-aroused sympathetic nervous system [...] drives you to become increasingly hypervigilant [...] In an effort to recognize, predict and avoid danger, hypervigilance is ingrained in your approach to being in the world. Hypervigilance narrows your attention into an incessant, on guard scanning of the people around you [...] and projects into the future[...][96]

The hypervigilant individual is not in his body because he's in yours, and indeed everybody else's. He's scanning the environment for danger, gauging your mood, trying to have some control over, or at least predict, what you'll do next. For him, "safety" depends on the mood states of others because he has no boundaries. And he has no boundaries because the natural sense of what is his, including his body, has been violated, and he has been trained that it is wrong to have a self—to have domain over his own embodied body.

> "Survivors now need to deconstruct this habit by working to stay more inside their own experience without constantly projecting their attention outward to read others."[97]

What is currently being learned about the vagus nerve is that it has multiple pathways with very different roles, originating in two different areas of the brainstem. Again, the newer part (the *ventral vagus*), is involved in normal human social behavior and the older part (the *dorsal vagus*) is involved in a primitive shut-down response to stress.

Porges, creator of The Polyvagal Theory, says that these different neural circuits support different ranges of behavior for mammals (including humans). "These systems work in harmony," Porges says, "to enable us to have good biological processes, but they also react to the world—we use them as defenses or responses to social challenges."[98]

The newer ventral vagus allows for the ability to communicate through facial expressions, vocalizations, and gestures via contingent social interactions. The importance of facial muscles in the preservation of safety and the avoidance of violence should not be underestimated. When this feature is actively engaged, charisma and resilience are highly evident. Porges describes the features of the most recently developed *ventral vagus*:

> There are people who make good eye contact, are curious of the other, and have broad range of facial expressivity. These people are also reciprocal in their social interactions. To maintain this reciprocity, they are literally throwing obvious and often subtle cues at each other. These cues have the potential to make the other person feel safe. When the cues are effective, the other person returns the cues through facial expressions and vocalizations. The face appears more alive, more expressive, the intonation of the voice becomes more prosodic, and the physical distance between the two people is often reduced as the physical space starts to approximate the reduced psychological distance.[99]

Part of what makes this intricately complicated system so mysterious is that the more primitive the operative system, the more power it has to hijack the overall function of the organism. According to Peter Levine,

> *It does this by inhibiting the more recent and more refined neurological subsystems, effectively preventing them from functioning. In particular, the immobilization system all but completely suppresses the social engagement/attachment system [...] The sympathetic nervous system also blocks the social engagement system, but not as completely as does the immobilization system [(dorsal vagus) which is the most primitive of the three defenses].[100]*

What is known about the vagus nerve and how it interfaces with our social and emotional health and experience is still not completely understood, even by the experts, but what we do know is that trauma and chronic lack of felt safety can result in imbalances, which are responsible for many different types of illness. In fact, many authorities on the subject argue that most ill health has problems with the regulation of the autonomic nervous system at its heart.[101] Symptoms and illnesses related to parasympathetic dominance include depression, low blood pressure, diabetes, low heart rate, slowed thinking, and hypoglycemia.[102]

According to many thinkers in the mindbody field, depending on our physiological state, we also experience the world differently. If our muscles are tight and constricted, we feel afraid. If we're breathing shallowly, our brain registers danger. If we're slumped, we feel not good enough. If we're silent, we feel like we don't matter. Our mental state (including our feelings and perceptions of things) is dependent on our physiological state. And our physiological state reflects our mental state. Polyvagal Theory offers evidence for what many of us already knew: we have some control over all of this. There are things we can do to help the parasympathetic nervous system strike a healthy balance with the sympathetic nervous system and calm the vagus nerve. And in doing so, we can have an impact on our mental/emotional state. What we are reaching for here is increased vagal tone, which results in an increased ability to self-regulate.

As mammals, humans are designed to use each other (and other mammals) to help them regulate their emotional state. Face-to-face interaction, for people who are calm enough, becomes a reciprocal way of self-regulating. This is something you can watch for in the facial tension of many mammals, including humans: the muscles around the eyes (that cause the crinkles) coincide with the inner ear muscles. When they are relaxed, we know that the individual is so relaxed that he has turned off his vigilance for predators. This is what Porges refers to as immobilization without fear, which can only occur following the establishment of "safety" via the social engagement system.[103]

For those of us with early relational trauma, it may be helpful to know that the surrender of relaxation in the arms of a beloved other has reliably signaled "life threat" to the nervous system. It's not your fault. It is developmental trauma. And there is evidence that you can repair it if you are motivated to do so. Intimate connection can have the safe and restorative function that stories and legends are built on. This will be the topic of the next chapter.

Beginning to Connect With the Body

In a relaxed-enough person, the sympathetic nervous system can be down-regulated and balanced by the PNS. But we can also take conscious, purposeful steps to enhance the normal parasympathetic functions of relaxation, revitalization, and regeneration. What follows is a list of activities that can facilitate the comfortable return to the body and, at the same time, help us to stay connected with a healthy sense of self. See what you think:

Ways to enhance the normal parasympathetic functions of relaxation, revitalization, and regeneration:

- Acquire some general knowledge about the autonomous nervous system (ANS)
- Breathe
  - Conscious breathing (diaphragmatic breathing)
  - Extending exhalation
  - Inhale, imagining a subtle energy moving from the top of your head, down to the base of your spine; Exhale, imagining the energy returning from the base of your spine and back up to the top of your head
- Use your voice (It stimulates the vagal system by vibrating it.)
  - Chant
  - Talk
  - Sing
  - Extend phrases while singing or speaking
- Listen
  - To the body, and notice and appreciate resonance
  - To individual sounds in music, in nature, in the environment
  - To others talking when it feels right
- Gently Correct Your Posture
  - Yoga
  - Tai Chi
  - Massage
  - Bodywork

- o CranioSacral Therapy
- o Physical Therapy
- Adopt Regular Habits and Mindsets
  - o Gratitude
  - o Visualization
  - o Meditation
- Touch and be touched

Product Features

What follows is a list of things the body is designed to do for us.

- Gives us form.
- Serves as a clear representation of a singular unit of beingness, in time and space.
- Carries us around from place to place.
- Allows us to take in sensory information from our environment.
- Allows us to interface with others and the world.
- Responds to attunement and gentleness by calming down.
- Responds to danger by contracting and dulling sensations of pain.
- Serves as a valuable source of instinctual information, supplementing logic and intelligence.
- Alerts us to natural early warning signs of real danger.
- Serves as a resource for self-knowledge, helping us to know ourselves, recognize our needs, desires, and limits.
- Helps us make safe, virtually instantaneous choices.
- Provides us and others with information about our emotional state.
- Offers abundant avenues for the expression of our authentic selves to others in the moment in subtle, conscious and unconscious ways.
- Serves as a vehicle for the movement and work of emotion.

Sure, there are lingering concerns about connecting, and here are some of the most common:

- Connecting is too painful.
- I'll fall apart. I can't handle my emotions.
- I can't—I don't know how.
- If I acknowledge my body, I'll have to deal with things in my past that I don't want to deal with.
- When I try to come back into my body after not living there, I am a stranger. It's uncomfortable.

Yes, it is quite possible that the sensations you've been avoiding are uncomfortable. At first, people often interpret them as pain. But if you leave it at that, you will turn down the road of managing and masking symptoms by taking medications, or otherwise trying to distract yourself from important information we'll now call sensation.

> *Advantages of being in my body include the allowing of myself to feel and move through/heal the uncomfortable emotion or sensation. And then the discomfort doesn't form a "knot" in my body. Having used massage for a few years now to help me feel more connected to my body, knots seem to form anytime I am resisting allowing myself to feel and process difficult emotions like heartbreak, anger, disappointment, etc. In these cases it feels as though I ignore my body altogether and try to operate from "above" or "outside."*
>
> *- Lu*

Lu helped me understand how important adequate tools are for being in the body. Gaining knowledge about how the body works, and tools to help us listen to it and care for it, give us a new perspective on sensation, transforming it into manageable information we can use to overcome our traumatic and stressful past. It connects us with our wisdom, and our strength, as we learn, integrate, appreciate, and embrace the parts of ourselves that we had formerly discarded.

> *My body seems to know things that my mind doesn't, usually related to trauma. I have noticed over several years that there are patterns to how my body feels/emotions related to the time of the year that something traumatic happened in my life that I have not clearly processed or allowed my body to fully feel and heal from.*
>
> *– Lu*

The information our bodies are designed to provide for us is vast and truly incredible. It is an unspeakable loss when we disconnect from this wise and honorable part of us. Pat Ogden, in her book, *Trauma and the Body*, says that "traumatized people characteristically lose the capacity to draw upon emotions as guides for action. They might suffer from alexithymia, a disturbance in the ability to recognize and find words for emotions."[104]

It has been said that knowledge is power. This truth couldn't be more relevant than it is in the area of embodiment. If we do not learn to use the sensory information available to us from our bodies, we have little awareness of our physical reaction to the stressors of the world and we become habituated to them. Then as we age, as a result of habituated responses, our joints can have the tendency to contract and draw in, resulting in less spaciousness between our ligaments, joints, bones, and tendons. This can certainly become a way of life for people, who by middle age (or even earlier) find themselves in pain and discomfort. The energy of suppressed and denied emotions and chronic muscular contraction eventually begin to manifest in the form of physical pain and discomfort. Craig Williamson calls this condition *dysfunctional kinesthesia*. The brain no longer consciously receives information coming in from the kinesthetic receptors of certain chronically stressed areas of the body, and you don't know why you have muscle pain because you cannot sense the degree of effort that your muscles are constantly making in attempts to protect and keep you safe. With dysfunctional kinesthesia, the brain has relinquished its ability to direct the muscles to relax correctly. Then because you have lost contact with the felt experience of these chronically tight muscles, you mistake their lack of responsiveness for weakness. He says,

> *If you have developed the ability to suppress your emotions [...] you may believe that the emotion simply goes away. In reality, it is* you *who goes away. The energy of the emotions still exists and still produces physiological effects.*[105]

Somatization of Emotions

What many researchers have found is that the human mind has ways of channeling emotions deemed unacceptable into physical reactions and physical symptoms. We can attend to these symptoms at any point in their development, but if they are chronically ignored, they can and do manifest as diseases such as arthritis, cancer, heart disease, Crohn's disease, Alzheimer's, diabetes, etc.

Somatization has to do with how our bodies take on and store the energy of our emotions when we don't allow that energy to flow through and/or enter our awareness. And we do this because in so many ways, our society teaches us that our emotions are wrong.

One very basic and universal form of somatization is the *drawing in* of the body. It is something the body naturally does in response to cold, loud noises, and large moving objects. When you see a person who is chronically drawn in, you make note at a conscious or unconscious level. That person appears to be frightened or cowering. And the subconscious mind takes in this information. *If they are not safe*, your proprioceptors will ask, *is there something I should be paying attention to here? Is there something I should fear?* Other forms of somatization include facial expressions. If grieving was not possible, a person may wear his or her grief in the form of an expression. On our orders, the body produces muscular tension to repress the sensation of the emotion. And in turn, tension restricts the flow of energy and our very awareness of the sensation of emotion.

Techniques such as CranioSacral Therapy and Reiki help bring awareness to emotions and tension held in the body, facilitate their release, and activate restorative parasympathetic function.

Somatic Experiencing, Hanna Somatics, Core Bodywork and Muscular Retraining are a few of the body therapy modalities that address the somatization of emotions by working with the body to regain connection with the sensations of chronically tensed muscles they can no longer feel or voluntarily relax. Due to overuse or constant contraction, the person is actually unable to sense that these muscles are overworked, or chronically contracted. Through the help of such therapies, the client once again becomes acquainted with these muscles, regains conscious control over them and reunites with the nuance that his or her body is capable of providing.

Medical Doctor John Sarno describes in his book, *Healing Back Pain: The Mind-Body Connection*, that what underlies much of the chronic pain his patients come to him for is "a command decision by the mind to produce a physical reaction rather than have the individual experience a painful emotion."[106] He has gained acclaim through his books and his treatment of chronic pain patients, which consists primarily of education. According to Sarno, the somatization of emotion happens when tension is habitually created in regions of the body, including their respective muscles, nerves, tendons, and ligaments, which then reduce flow of blood and cause mild oxygen deprivation, resulting in pain. In his list of ways that Tension Myositis Syndrome (TMS) can show up in our lives, Sarno includes: peptic ulcer, spastic colitis, constipation, tension headache, migraine headache, cardiac palpitations, eczema , allergic rhinitis (hay fever), prostratitis, ringing in the ears, dizziness, laryngitis, pathological dry mouth, frequent urination, and many others.[107] He urges people to examine possible emotional causes for pain alongside any care they receive from their medical doctor, and to search for causes instead of merely treating symptoms.

Body Phobia

Generalized body phobia is another largely unconscious reason people are resistant to connecting with and embracing their bodies. It should come as no surprise that people often feel a lot of shame and/or hatred toward their bodies. Our society teaches people from a very young age that their bodies are naturally defective. If you care to look deeper, you can see on so many levels how people are still led to believe that their bodies are inherently evil.

The word carnal was one that came up with great frequency in the church where I grew up. I don't remember looking this word up in the dictionary, or thinking about it, consciously. But when I began to consider the reasons why people might disconnect, I decided to do a little digging—for a definition that reflects what I absorbed from that time. Poking around on the Internet, I

141

found it—the thought pattern that imprinted on my consciousness as I grew up in my parents' spiritual community.

> *CARNAL: In this fallen state [all men] are subject to the lusts, passions, and appetites of the flesh. They are spiritually dead, having been cast out of the presence of the Lord; and thus "they are without God in the world, and they have gone contrary to the nature of God." They are in a "carnal state" (Alma 41:10-11); they are of the world. Carnality connotes worldliness, sensuality, and inclination to gratify the flesh. (Mormon Doctrine, p.113)[108]*

My parents were not Mormons, but on this subject, the sentiment is indistinguishable. As a young child, not only was I terrified about becoming overwhelmed because of intense feelings I had no help navigating, but I was encouraged by my family's spiritual community to cut myself off from my body, because of its antipathy with God. I wonder how anyone growing up in such a church could have a healthy attitude toward the body, sensuality or physical pleasure. Here's what I found at Dictionary.com:

> Carnal – adj. 1) pertaining to or characterized by the flesh or the body, its passions and appetites; sensual: *carnal pleasures*; 2) not spiritual; merely human; temporal; worldly: *a man of secular, rather carnal, leanings.*[109]

Synonyms include: bodily, lustful, lecherous, lascivious, libidinous, concupiscent. The word itself casts judgment in an unambiguous, though underhanded kind of way. It does not directly say *"bad,"* or *"evil,"* but instead *"of the flesh,"* or *"worldly,"* which were words I heard spat or whispered, rather than spoken, sending a very clear message of shame in our home, signaling the unspoken message: **Don't ask**. *Decent people do not engage in carnal activities or pleasures,* was what I took away.

It isn't surprising to me, then, that with some people, even the use of the word *body* is a trigger. For many, the word is loaded with meaning that is still not explored—possibly stemming from past violations, or the disconnect or shame their parents felt about sexuality or their own bodies.

> *"Being in my body is a lot of work. I don't like it. Why does it have to hurt?" "I just want this discomfort to go away. My discomfort brings others discomfort. I want them to experience peace."*
>
> - Lu

Mindfulness

The items that make up the list of ways to connect with the body (above) all involve a practice called mindfulness. Mindfulness is a practice that helps us learn to activate the Watchtower, which, if you remember, is the medial prefrontal cortex—the only part of the brain that we can actually use to consciously interface with the autonomic nervous system. Mindfulness allows us to increase our ability to be here now. It allows us to utilize the information coming in from our senses, both outside us and inside us. It enhances our ability to engage in interoception, which is the ability to direct our attention toward our organism, to the functioning of our inner landscape, to attune to movement, tension, temperature, etc., and receive information about our emotional world. Mindfulness has been shown definitively to reduce physical and psychological pain and increase capacity for emotion regulation. It is in using mindfulness and increasing interoception that we learn about nuance.

143

Grounding

Grounding is a loose term that might be considered more a byproduct of being connected to the body than an actual technique. However, grounding can often be achieved through visualizing sending roots into the earth, or using a grounding cord to allow the energy of emotions to pass out of the body and into the earth. In *Language of Emotions*, Karla McLaren explains the function of grounding: "When you can ground your tension and any intense emotions, you won't need to blast other people or repress everything and become flattened."[110] She recommends the practice as an invaluable means for managing emotions and living a more fully integrated life. Physiologically, she explains, emotion involves the movement of energy. Learning that we can allow the energy to move through us and that it has not actually come to stay, is one of the most basic but important things we can learn about emotions. In the passage below, Karla describes her experience of being ungrounded, and the benefits she receives from grounding.

> *Grounding is the opposite of dissociation; when I was a dissociator and I felt discomfort in my body, I'd lift away and leave my body behind. I did nothing whatsoever with the discomfort—I just flew away. With grounding, I listen to my body, I help it deal with discomfort or upsetting things, and I take charge of the situation. I don't just run away and leave my body to deal with discomfort all by itself. When I ground myself, I integrate the village inside me.*[111]

Lu also describes groundedness and how it compares to dissociation.

The feeling of groundedness that comes from being in my body is a very anchored, present awareness—a feeling of being supported (in my particular experience) by something firmly behind me, protecting me. The advantage of being in my body is that when I am in my body, I can allow it to feel; I can heal by allowing the uncomfortable emotion or sensation to move through, and heal. When I'm not in my body, I don't feel the emotions. Instead of feeling them, the discomfort forms a "knot" in my body. Having used massage for a few years to help me feel more connected to my body, I came to understand that knots seem to form anytime I am resisting allowing myself to feel and process difficult emotions like heartbreak, anger, disappointment, etc.

When I have resisted feeling (disconnecting) in the past, it feels as though I ignore my body altogether and try to operate from "above" or "outside". If I do not allow myself to be connected/grounded to my body, I notice my awareness anchors right above my head, almost as if it is attempting to ignore the fact that my body is feeling something.[112]

Touch

Finally, lack of physical contact contributes to actual, measurable health problems, particularly in early childhood, but also for adults. In a study of baby rhesus monkeys, back in 1975, James Prescott found a stronger drive for physical comfort than for food.[113] And if one is aware, steps can be taken to meet this physical need. A minimum of 10 minutes of close physical contact every day can make a measurable difference when it comes to stress management. If you are not partnered, you can

145

benefit from cuddling with yourself, or even cradling yourself as you would a baby. Hugging, holding or being held, dancing, taking a leisurely shower or a bath, giving or receiving a massage, and so on are all ways you can meet your touch quota, while letting your body know you appreciate it. Having and caring for a pet can also help meet this need. Notice the effect any amount of physical touch and conscious, loving attention has on your level of stress and on your felt sense of your body. If you can slow down enough, you will notice that such care and indulgence is not only enjoyable, but that it also serves to help your body relax and rejuvenate.

Healing Trauma

The general consensus among attachment researchers is that we cannot effectively address trauma, especially early relational trauma, without paying attention to the body. "The single most important issue for traumatized people," says Bessel van der Kolk, "is to find a sense of safety in their own bodies."[114]

When trauma is properly addressed, our bodily memories become personal history. We are no longer held in the grip of a never-ending feeling of crisis or danger. We are no longer victims. With the release of these memories comes the release of all the hooks and triggers that have haunted us for all these years, randomly catapulting us into hypervigilance, regression, re-enactment and dysfunction.

There are a great many excellent resources at our disposal. Mindfulness practices and listening are the ones that are available to virtually everyone. According to Peter Levine, "Advances in trauma treatment involve spending time being very silent: listening to messages from your body and noticing how your body is living."[115] Beyond these simple practices that you can implement yourself is the world of body-mind practitioners and their wealth of experience and knowledge. These include but are certainly not limited to:

- **EMDR Phases 1-2** Installing positive resources with the help of bilateral tapping is a part of EMDR preparation and resource development. Through this approach, a therapist can help install resources that were not present for the individual in his or her childhood, but can still be imagined. They include but are not limited to: peaceful places, nurturing figures, protective figures, wise figures, positive memories of strength and success, of health or of wholeness. Developing imagery around such resources and adding tapping is a way to strengthen and enhance the felt sense of safety and groundedness so that trauma processing can occur.[116]

- **The therapeutic relationship itself** is the most effective tool therapists have for healing relational trauma. The ongoing relationship provides the client with opportunities to interact, have emotional experiences with the presence and support of another, and to build trust. To the extent to which the therapist is attuned, connecting, resonant and present—adjusting what he or she is doing according to the client's needs—this is creating new neural pathways in the client's brain. These moments of healing have the potential to change the whole nervous system.

- **When we can't put our experience into words**, whether due to the individual's developmental stage at the time of the traumatic experience, or some other difficulty finding the language to tell the story, there are CranioSacral Therapy, Somatic Therapies, Movement, Art, and Expressive Therapies.

- **Somatic Countertransference.** This is a concept addressed beautifully by David Wallin, in which a practitioner uses his or her own felt sense to help understand what is happening for the client. Somatic countertransference emphasizes the use of the therapist's sensations and awareness when working with a client who is having trouble connecting with their emotional experience during session.

  > I refer to it as somatic countertransference—what's going on in the therapist's body[...] In therapy, dissociated experience is often an experience the patient can't put into words, or an experience that can't even be put into thoughts or feelings. My attention often is on what is being evoked in me, because I think what people can't own and articulate, they often evoke in others. I've also got my attention on what's being enacted between me and the patient, since that's another way in which dissociated experience gets expressed.[117]

In Conclusion

We can give our bodies what we needed and yearned for as infants and children if we take the time to tune in. As outlined in Chapter 3, a child needs touch, attunement in the form of resonant connection and relational dialog, he needs to be seen, he needs consistency and predictability, he needs unconditional love and acceptance, permission to have needs, permission to say no, and modeling of healthy adult interactions. A child experiences very real consequences of not having any or all of these things. And what's essential for you to know now is that if you were that child, these consequences are reversible. Not only that, but that you are reversing them right now, by learning to parent the body. Being a parent to the body means being attuned to these truly defenseless parts of us that are fully reliant on our care, just as we were completely dependent on our parents' care when we first came into the world.

Chapter 5 - Healthy Adult Intimacy

As a species, our motivations for adult intimacy have changed over the past several centuries, as our culture and our world have changed, and as we have evolved. Accordingly, we need to make adjustments to better understand what intimacy is for. Where *making family* has served as a mechanism for survival in the past, our interactions with others have become more a potential for life enhancement. We don't need a primary partner for our happiness, or even to procreate, but we do need other people in order to get the most out of life.

Looking back at my own forays into intimate relationships, I see an interesting push-me-pull-you-type energy: an aching for intimacy, while holding a potential partner at a distance; both feeling incomplete without a partner and an unnamable foreboding that the instant I formed a monogamous bond, I would begin to lose my self—a less-than-conscious resentment toward my partner that manifested as a dogged resistance to being pleased. It has not been until very recently that I began to think about attachment in terms of my parents, and to draw the parallels I have had with men with regard to bonding, safety, and selfhood.

Dave Richo, in his book *Daring to Trust*, says, "Attachment, in psychology, refers to our natural desire for physical and emotional closeness to another person. It happens through engaging with one another and responding to one another. Attachment does not mean possessiveness or control but rather engagement and responsiveness by showing the five A's [attention, acceptance, appreciation, affection, and allowing]. It is not compulsive clinging, with obsessive thoughts and a gnawing insatiability. Those are the three elements that signal addiction in the psychological realm. They are also what define suffering in the Buddhist teaching on attachment."[118]

Various similarities stand out among happy, successful couples. These things are reflected in great literature and are assumed to be what normal relationships are made of. Happy couples regard their unions with mutuality, deep commitment, kindness, and respect. The culture they create together is playful, safe and nourishing. In his important book, *Wired For Love: How Understanding Your Partner's Brain and Attachment Style Can Help You Defuse Conflict and Build a Secure Relationship,* Stan Tatkin refers to healthy attachment as a tether. He says, "Partners who create and maintain a tether to one another experience more personal safety and security, have more energy, take more risks and experience overall less stress than couples who do not."[119]

This tethering is the idea I'd like to talk about first, as the primary connection or bond that can be (but isn't always) created between partners. In *Wired for Love*, Tatkin describes what he calls a "couple bubble," in which a couple can agree to certain principles which guide their attitudes, behaviors and priorities, and actually allow them to "build synergy in [their] relationships, such that [they] are able to operate together in ways that are greater than if [they] each lived as essentially separate individuals."[120]

While it's hard to argue the advantages of primary partnership, I have some practical concerns. People who have not recovered from relational trauma 1) do not bring their full, embodied selves to the relationship because they do not know how, and 2) do not have the social or emotional development necessary to agree on the principles and comport themselves accordingly. One need not look far to see the relationships that create more stress than they relieve; that leave their members doubting their value, feeling unsure, unsafe, and unlovable. The life-enhancing bond remains elusive, and the requisites for creating and supporting it are nowhere to be found. The couples who find themselves in this unfortunate situation match or mirror one another in their unpreparedness; neither of them can understand what is actually going on, and so it is beyond their capability to support one another and create this protective bubble. It goes without saying that the environment of these unions is anything but safe.

I, for one, am seeing the importance of setting aside primary partnership *with another person* as a goal. Instead, my focus is on tending and nurturing and strengthening my sense of self so that at some point in the future I can have the social and emotional development necessary to stay embodied when I am in partnership with a close, intimate other. This chapter will highlight the elements of forging a relationship with the self, through the use of the information that is available from the body.

In *Wired for Love*, Stan Tatkin distinguishes between three attachment styles (Anchors, Islands, and Waves), which shape the different kinds of dances people engage in in their relationships. Anchors, he says, readily attach and are able to navigate healthy relationships. Anchors characterize the ability to form a *secure* bond with an intimate partner.

As we have already discussed, insecure attachment is a result of complex trauma. Tatkin divides people with insecure attachment styles into Islands and Waves. *Islands*, he says, often feel intruded upon by others. They often feel trapped, and out of control in response to closeness. They fear too much intimacy and discount the value of being soothed, comforted or protected by someone else. They prefer to have control, i.e., *If I withdraw first, I don't have to worry about being abandoned.*

*Wave*s, by contrast, fear being abandoned by a partner. They experience discomfort in response to being left alone for too long. They commonly feel that they are a burden in relationships, and they are overly sensitized to the anticipation of rejection. They want to be tethered, but either don't expect it in return or are unwilling to give it in return.

For those of you who are already in committed relationships, continue to develop and explore your couple bubble. Knowing your attachment styles can help you better navigate conflict and create more harmony in your relationship. For two people actively working toward safety in relationship, committed partnership has the potential for profound healing, growth and evolution.

Obviously, not everyone has the same set of needs when it comes to safety. And what is important to remember is that our relationships in adulthood are completely elective; it is our responsibility to decide what does and does not work for us. We're in charge of that. If we have tried, and have not experienced safety and comfort in intimate relationships, it is okay to admit that. And it is okay to change up the strategy.

For those of us who are in the early stages of recovering from developmental trauma, the couple bubble may not be the best laboratory for exploration and growth. In the following sections we'll look at how we might begin to bridge these developmental gaps and discern when and how to enter a safe bubble and achieve the benefits that enduring partnership provides.

As we tell our stories about what happened to us, as we are heard and seen, as we identify and expand our ability to tolerate our emotions, and as we become more attuned to what we like and do not like, our unique self becomes more defined, more solid, and more known. Once we have begun this work, we begin to nurture a sense of committed connectedness to ourselves. Such connectedness could be conceptualized as a safety zone or a cocoon. Tatkin helps *couples* develop a safety zone to ensure safety in the environment of the partnership. He describes it as a "mutually constructed membrane cocoon, or womb that holds a couple together and protects each partner from outside elements."[121] For the purposes of forging a secure bond *with oneself*, we can modify this idea just a little. The purpose of the "*intra*personal bubble" is to contain and protect the development of a secure relationship with our vulnerable bodies. Just as a couple needs to attune and re-attune to maintain the safety and commitment of the relationship, an individual needs to attune and re-attune with his or her body and be receptive to the information that it provides in order to forge a fully embodied self. Using Tatkin's model as a starting place, the following is a list of things that need to happen to keep our "intrapersonal bubble" healthy and intact.

- Take the time to re-attune after separation. If you find yourself disconnected, tense, or feeling "off," check in with yourself to see if you have any pressing needs, i.e., am I thirsty, angry, triggered, tired?
- Use body awareness to see where you are holding tension, and take steps to release it.
- Attune to your emotional state. Becoming conscious of your emotions helps allow you to stay in the here and now, and make continual use of real-time sensory information, rather than shifting into past emotional states and essentially reliving relational or other trauma through a triggered state. This information is readily available to you if you can stay calm enough to access it. Simply by observing yourself, you can make assessments about your emotional state based on muscle tension, energy level, breath and voice quality.
- Develop an up-to-date owner's manual for your various parts. It is quite possible that a part of you is comfortable with the idea of meeting someone new, for instance, and another part of you is literally terrified of the prospect. Taking some time to study these parts (or any parts you might have) and understanding what you need to do to stay connected with your larger purpose and goals— while treating each of these parts with the care and respect they deserve—is another strategy that can help you stay in the here and now; to ride out a potentially overwhelming situation without needing to shut your feelings down or to dissociate and abandon your body and your felt sense.

In the intrapersonal bubble, the emphasis is on being sensitive to the parts of you that have been chronically dissociated, or the parts that you have kept pressed out of awareness. When you have a more developed relationship with yourself, you will learn

155

to benefit from the wisdom, vision and gifts of these parts that you have been dismissing. In this way, not only will these formerly exiled parts be accepted and cared for, but they will help you see and appreciate the richest and most *uniquely you* aspects of your self.

Strategies to Avoid Intimacy

As we heal, we can more easily recognize the behaviors we have engaged in that made healthy intimacy so unattainable for us in the past. Maybe for some of you, the idea of intimacy as a trigger is a stretch. But if for you early intimacy brought with it a loss or threat so great that it constitutes trauma (even if you can't quite wrap your mind around that quite yet), then you have naturally developed strategies that will help prevent you from having to feel those feelings of terror, loss, dependency, and/or vulnerability ever again. What follows is a list of the covert strategies to avoid intimacy I have encountered in myself and through my work with clients:

- Addictions and compulsions
  - Process addictions
  - Substance addictions
  - Co-dependency (addiction to a person who "isn't okay" without you)
- Perfectionism (Unrealistic Expectations—Judgment of Self and Others)
  - My outputs must be above average.
  - The people I associate with must be exceptional (because they are a reflection of me).
- Hiding behind a mask of virtue or self-righteousness based on values we learned from our parents (which are largely unconscious), in order to feel safe and accepted.
  - I produce (I have value because of what I do).

- I have no needs (I'm not a burden on anyone; I carry my own weight).

I am in the process of cutting through my defenses against intimacy, and forging a secure bond with my self, from which I can count on safety, support, comfort, and unconditional love. I have learned to recognize (at least after the fact), how I inadvertently hand my power over to another person. When I can recognize it, I can then step back, re-member my power, and choose again. I am learning to distinguish the seduction of a vague or unrealistic promise from the steady groundedness of my own felt sense, and to take great pleasure in knowing that this is what home and safety is for me.

But this is a slow and gradual process. For those of us who are newly developing a stronger sense of self, and have habitually disconnected from our own emotions when in the presence of a close, intimate other, infatuation can be a very confusing thing. That all-encompassing feeling of falling in love tends to be so similar to primordial love—the body of our mother. It's no wonder the person who has experienced developmental trauma succumbs to a trancelike slumber when he or she finds that attentive other—when infatuation triggers us to hand our hearts and our power over. But the nature of this spark of infatuation is not to stay, and afterwards we are left to deal with the nitty gritty of this person we have summoned into our lives, and to whom we have pledged our hearts. By that point, the best thing we can do is to return to the present with as much consciousness and love as possible, and reconnect with our selves. That means showing up as who we really are instead of who we think you will like, in order to make you stay.

As an insecurely attached child, I learned it was safer not to trust, as my needs for belonging, safety, and support were not well met. As an adult, I've found the idea of allowing another person to earn my respect, trust, and affection over time extremely seductive. But seduction is based on illusion and fantasy; unrealistic expectations that emerge from unresolved early relational trauma. It is not a good substitute for experience-informed wisdom or body-informed knowledge. And through much trial and error, I am in the process of learning how to stay conscious and connected—when I am sitting or standing across from another living, breathing person—to my felt sense, to pay attention to my physical responses to people and situations, and thereby stay connected with my own inner compass. This allows me to know, more readily, what is and is not acceptable or desirable to me.

After a person has begun to feel secure in his or her ability to remain embodied and in integrity with the self for some time, the question of healthy partnering may come up for consideration once more. What seems to keep so many people coming back is the hope that experience and healing can change our wiring so that we can safely relax into the deliciousness of a sustainable partnered union. The following is my best attempt at a checklist for primary partnership readiness.

Checklist for Relationship Readiness
- Unambiguous desire for primary partnership
- Self knowledge about our personal relational style, and whether having a partner makes sense for us
- Clarity about what we desire, need and expect from a partner
- The willingness to self advocate. Also known as fighting, this allows the partner to experiment with and learn through engagement how to manage his or her own power, and activates the mental and emotional muscles

necessary to negotiate for his or her self-interests (more on this later).

- Ability to attune to your emotional state *and* to that of another person. Emotional attunement is a state of consciousness that allows you and another person to stay in the here and now during interactions so that continual use of real-time sensory information can be made, and regression avoided. Real-time information is readily available to you if you can stay calm enough to access it. Simply by observing yourself and the other person, you can make assessments about emotional state based on auditory, visual and kinesthetic cues.

More on Self Advocacy

Members of a committed partnership need to bring their self-interests to the relationship. I call this *self advocacy*; Tatkin calls it *fighting*. "Couples who are in it for the long haul know how to play and fight well, remain fearlessly confident in the resilience of their relationship, and don't try to avoid conflict." Tatkin says that while self-interests are a necessary given, they exist as part of the greater good of the relationship, such that, "when a fight occurs, nobody loses and everybody wins." [122]

Smart fighting, Tatkin says, is "about wrestling with your partner, engaging without hesitation or avoidance, and at the same time being willing to relax your own position. You go back and forth with each other, until the two of you come up with something that's good for both of you. You take what you each bring to the table and, with it, create something new that provides mutual relief and satisfaction."[123]

Emerging from a life marked by relational trauma, we each have our automatic response: the one that worked for us when we were young. For me it was freeze, fawn and eventual flight. I forfeited the "fight" reflex, having watched my sister being

159

punished and beaten down for using hers. Having defaulted to freeze and fawn so automatically, I missed out on the opportunity to experiment with and develop the other possible responses that would have allowed me to maintain equilibrium in my relationships.

Violence and Abuse

Whether you intend to heal your relational trauma from childhood or nurture a deep and authentic relationship with another person, you owe it to yourself to immediately eliminate all threatening behavior from your internal and external environment. John Gottman of the Gottman Institute[124] and Tatkin agree that contempt is one of the biggest threats to relationships. Contempt includes expression of disgust, disrespect, condescension, and sarcasm. It should come as no surprise that these attitudes, when directed toward the self or the body, would threaten an individual's self-esteem and sense of self-worth, and ultimately undermine his or her interactions with intimate others.

Think about this next list in terms of how you treat yourself (in a stressful situation) *and* past unsuccessful relationships. Think also about relationships you witnessed as you were growing up. Tatkin considers all of the following to be threatening behaviors:

- Raging
- Hitting or other forms of physical violence
- Threats against the relationship
- Threats against the person
- Threats against others important to the person
- Holding on for too long and not letting go
- Refusing to repair or make right a wrong
- Withdrawing for periods longer than 1-2 hours
- Behaving habitually in an unfair or unjust manner

- Putting ego-based interests ahead of the relationship too much of the time
- Expressing contempt (devaluation: e.g., "You're a moron.")
- Expressing disgust (loathing or repulsion; e.g., "You make me sick.")[125]

Denying or trying to "get rid of" parts of yourself including the body and its needs and feelings is a form of violence. Refusing to forgive yourself for not being perfect is another form of self-abuse. And remaining disconnected from the self, the body and its needs and feelings is a form of self-abandonment and neglect. Being harsh and unrelenting and expecting things that aren't realistic from our bodies is a form of violence as well. If the culture of our internal environment includes self-violence and abuse, this is the very first thing that needs to change.

Can You Be Pleased?

I cannot move more deeply into the topic of healthy adult intimacy until I share another anecdote. A couple years into my Mexico adventure, after connecting and reconnecting with myself, connecting and reconnecting with an enduring faith that I am here to experience joy and pleasure, I remember walking along the streets of the city, feeling deeply pleasured. I remember noticing how the smile on my lips came from deep within, how the life I was experiencing and the things that came together to form it were profoundly pleasing to me. I'm not sure what I was so pleased about in the moment, but it may have had something to do with the abundance of time I had, the freedom to prioritize my use of it, and the knowing I had that I was taken care of. Mind you, I'm living with little more than the clothes on my back and a place to stack my books and plug in my computer.

I remember thinking that if Spirit—or God—was my lover, that He/She must have found me to be a pretty tough cookie in decades past. Not that I was not grateful, but that pleasure was really not that high on my list of priorities. I thought about couples, and hypothetical men who were with wives who were not receptive to their attempts to please them. I thought about that lucky man whose woman could be deeply and thoroughly pleased, and the type of woman she might be—and how the angels might be singing right now because I could be so affected by and receptive of their gifts.

What was undoubtedly adding to my entertainment was thinking about how unexplainable all this happiness was: the fact that I had just—due to the unsolicited kindness of my landlord—graduated from a cotton mat on the floor to an ancient wooden bed whose slats would periodically fall to the floor with a clatter if I moved too much or too suddenly while upon it. And this was also a time when I shared a kitchen with a small family who believed that dishwashing was a somewhat extraneous or unnecessary activity. At the age of 51, I had an income that from one month to the next had me wondering if my expenses would be met without overdraft charges. How lovely though, the thought that I was among *those* people— those women who could be pleased—who received pleasure, who felt gratitude deeply for what they had consciously asked for, which, for me, was time and freedom and travel. Truly, the gifts extended far beyond what I had asked for. It was not difficult to be grateful. Receptivity, then, as I move into this material, is such an important ingredient. The ability to receive with pleasure—an act that is inexplicably related to the ability to desire and tolerate joy.

Advocating for the Body

Embodiment is about having a *relationship* with the body. In our criteria for healthy relationships above, we include mutuality, deep commitment, kindness, and respect. The inner culture of a happily embodied person, according to this set of criteria, would be playful, safe and nourishing. So having a relationship with your body not only has to do with respect and physical care, but also curiosity and receptiveness because the body holds the information we need to help us figure out what we want and what we need from moment to moment.

Forging a relationship with my body is a process that allows me to do for myself what I critically needed and didn't get from my adult caretakers in my first three years of life. And with it comes the emergence of a stronger, more resilient sense of self that can stay in integrity, even in close proximity with others. It is my hope that as you learn about your body and what it can do, you will experience a natural upwelling of willingness to advocate for it.

Advocating well for the body requires four things. The first is a *willingness* to listen to or attend to the body and its needs; the second is becoming an expert at what pleases, comforts and delights you. The third is the voicing of your perspective in the world to facilitate the achievement of your goals and desires and to re-establish safety and comfort when necessary. And the fourth is taking concrete steps in the direction of your heart's desires. To recap, advocacy for the body involves:

- Willingness to listen or attend to your body and its needs
- Becoming an expert on what pleases, comforts and delights you (a discernment that needs to draw heavily on information from the body, but may also require negotiation between mental and physical perspectives)

163

- Voicing your perspective in the world to facilitate the achievement of your goals and desires and to re-establish safety when necessary
- Taking concrete steps in the direction of your heart's desires (information gathering, asking for help, experimenting, making important decisions, walking away from things that are no longer working)

It should come as no surprise that advocating for the body is self parenting. And the emergence of a strong sense of self (also known as individuation or psychological birth) is a result of these steps. In my experience, the process needs to be facilitated by or can be greatly accelerated with the help of an experienced coach or counselor.

Addressing Unmet Childhood Needs as Adults

According to the Weinholds, "[P]eople whose social and emotional needs aren't met in the first three years of their lives carry them around. These needs then emerge in adult relationships and interfere with intimacy. This is the chief cause of counter-dependent behaviors in adults. When individuals simply do not get their developmental needs met in childhood, they find themselves just 'playing grown-up.' [...] Counter-dependent behaviors help you cope with having unmet needs."[126]

Finding the Words

Thinking back on the relationships in my life that I designated as "intimate," I sensed the person was there, but I also sensed that meaningful, relevant support, connection (attunement), and warmth were not naturally forthcoming, and that asking for these things would not have yielded a desired result. Ultimately, their being "there" did not provide a sense of safety beyond, perhaps, constricted and incidental economic support... sometimes. With words like these, I can use this information to inform my investigation of my felt experience as a child. Though my mind remembers very little, my body can fill in a lot.

Among the few childhood memories I have are the ones in which I am feeling overwhelmed, confused and inadequate, and not knowing how to ask for help. Conclusions I drew from that experience might have been, *There is no help for me. I'm on my own. It is not mine to be supported, but to provide support.* These are the beliefs I unknowingly brought into my adult relationships.

How about you? Was your first attachment figure a consistent source of comfort and reassurance to you? Were you adequately attuned to her? Were your needs for healthy adult interaction and role modeling met? When you think of yourself in your mother's arms, does your body melt and relax? Or are you unable to picture it? Does your mind race and your body tense up, go on high alert? If this is the case for you, you were not securely attached to your mother. And chances are, you have brought this way of being in the world to your adult relationships.

As you continue to do your emotional work, you will become more and more aware of your bodily responses to people and your environment. Some people will have one impact on you, while other people will have another. As you learn, you will be able to increasingly use your felt sense as an indicator of whether you actually like the person you are with.

Another thing to be aware of is that some of us associate intimacy, in general, with a heightened state of vigilance; the flood of adrenaline, the expenditure of mental energy that has an almost compulsive feel to it. As you tend to and heal your early relational trauma, you will increasingly sense, at a body level, that intimacy is the refuge it was designed to be, and your mind will begin to slow down. Just being in the company of your beloved will become more natural, and put you more at ease.

In this journey toward embodiment, it is not necessary to make anyone wrong, least of all our parents. But it is important to search out the words, and give ourselves a conscious, embodied voice, nonetheless. I encourage you to give it a try, approaching the process of naming what happened to you with as much curiosity and compassion as possible, knowing that it is a necessary prerequisite to finally overcoming trauma; to coming home and being accepted into the tribe. It's okay. Doing this work in the privacy of your own home will not hurt anyone.

Being Received

Nurturing friendships is an adult way of responding to the real need for connection. Not as potential business partners, or as potential clients, or with the intention of getting work done or accomplishing anything in particular, but with the primary purpose of experiencing the company of the other. The presence that only another human can provide serves as the third and final stage of initiation—the medicine that connects an initiate to the unique strengths, maturity and gifts he or she has come to share in the world.

An astute friend from college noticed that I had a tendency to collect "exceptionally bright and gifted people" and keep them as friends. Owning this past tendency, I can understand my younger self and my hopes that my friendships might withstand the tests of my ego defenses, which would inevitably rear their heads when feelings of inadequacy, fear or vulnerability showed up in the relationship. What else was there to hold a friendship together, besides admiration and worthiness based on what one could do?

My friend Renee could make pies. She was not a virtuoso violinist. She listened when I needed to talk. She was there when I was bored and needed adult stimulation in the fishbowl that was our Dexter trailer park in rural Missouri when our children were babies. She was there when I was leaving my first husband. She ended up leaving an imprint on my soul: *This is what adult friends feel like. This is what friends do.* I didn't realize it then, but I was connecting with my felt need for companionship, for attention, for continuity, for attunement and acceptance. In Renee's humble kitchen I felt met while meeting myself; I explored myself in the context of another person. My marriage did not offer me that.

Entering and exiting dysfunctional relationships—which was a strong feature of my twenties, thirties and forties—can be a very absorbing thing. And as a result, I left a lot of important developmental needs on the sidelines. When the dust started to clear, however, and there was an opening to think about what was actually important to me, I was finally able to put this into words, too. I value quality connection. Connecting deeply with others is important to me. But I noticed that I had not spent much time at all nurturing friendships. In fact, I wasn't really sure how it was supposed to be done.

These days, I have consciously made the decision to make friendship an important part of my life. I've had the great fortune to meet people with whom I've sensed a quality in our relating that I wanted more of; a balance of giving and receiving that felt healthy and nourishing to me. I've had sufficient positive regard for myself to afford the time necessary to nurture my friendships, and through these friendships, over time, I enjoy, I learn, I notice how I feel, and I grow. I am so grateful for my friends. My friends don't need to be somehow exceptionally bright or gifted—though they always are. They just need to be themselves. And what makes them my friends is this felt sense of comfort and joy and pleasure and safety that I notice during most of our interactions. The feeling of lightness and happiness I get when I anticipate the possibility of a visit.

As I go about exploring this new corridor of thought— friendship—I follow the information that is available to me through my felt sense. If it feels good, I look forward to our next visit. If it doesn't, then I get to see if this is a friendship that is going to last over time. Those friendships that do withstand the test of time come with a feeling I got with Renee—a feeling of being cared about, included; met with curiosity and heart. It is a feeling of being somewhat known, and knowing another.

With these friendships, I can also count on this interaction— though mostly positive, affirming, and easy—to sometimes offer me challenges, which I have the incentive to work through. When this working-through happens, the relationship is strengthened and deepened—or it weakens and prunes itself over time, if our differences are just too great and unresolvable. And so we have a pleasant and safe context in which to experience intense feelings and grow. When we're conscious and skilled enough, we can wait until the intensity of our emotions has passed, before we do irreparable damage. We can give ourselves the time we need to return to the present when we get triggered. After we've had a chance to think and reconnect with our deeper values, we can respond with presence, thoughtfulness, honesty and kindness. If we do regress and act in unkind or inappropriate ways, we have a chance to own what we have done, to apologize and make amends, and when this happens, it's another opportunity to test and strengthen trust and the bonds of the friendship.

The successful nurturing of friendships does require a basic value that having friends is worthwhile, that people are trustworthy enough to merit our time, and that connecting with others is edifying and enjoyable. For many people who have experienced relational trauma, they are not completely sure that the world is a safe place and that people are trustworthy. For many, at least on an unconscious level, people are not safe, can't be trusted, or are going to abandon or betray us in one way or another. When this is the case, we will experience our friendship through this filter.

Because of an underlying belief that friends were going to abandon or betray me, I have used strategies to protect myself. My "favorite" one has been perfectionism. Any friend I had would fall under my scrutiny (read sabotage) and somehow not be quite good enough just based on who they were and the fact that we had caught each other's attention. This is probably why I apparently had the habit of collecting somehow exceptionally bright and gifted people as friends—in attempts to boost my self-esteem and ensure that the friendships could withstand the trials I was about to put them through.

In my 50s, what I'm learning about adult friendship is that other people are different from me. The advantage I have at this stage in my life is that I really *get* that we all have separate brains, and separate pasts. We've drawn separate conclusions about the world. Although some of these variables are likely to line up between us, we are not going to agree on everything. Without a strong sense of self, self-awareness, and understanding of emotions and needs, friendships are going to blow up in our faces, and we often have to jettison them without looking back.

Even if we agree on a conscious level, we may have unexamined values and beliefs that are at odds with our conscious ones. These unexamined values and beliefs are the things that will come at us with greatest intensity in our most intimate relationships, but we can count on them to come up in our friendships as well. In the arena of friendships, where the stakes are not as high, and the intensity not so great, we have the opportunity to let them play out, thus bringing them into consciousness so we have a chance to examine them and make necessary adjustments, if we are willing.

Another little relic from childhood that is going to stand in the way of rewarding friendships is how I feel about me. If I have an undercurrent of low self-esteem or self-loathing, I am going to project that onto any friends or intimates I associate with long enough. This is just how it works, and I suspect that is why my parents didn't value friendship in the way I am describing here. For them, "friendship" was an extra and, in the culture of one crisis after another, it did not have much of a place.

I am still learning how to be aware of emotions as they arise, and to allow their felt sense to enter my conscious awareness so they can inform my behavior and choices. Staying connected with my felt sense is such an important part of making feelings a normal part of my everyday life. It helps allow me to recognize the differences between me and my loved ones. I catch myself more quickly when I slip into projecting images of my "perfect," conditionally loved self onto you. I more often approach you with open curiosity, knowing that your experience is in many ways different from mine. How other people are, how they cope, and their emotions are also not mine to tend, change or control. You feel how you feel. I feel how I feel. And in the arena of finding good friends and nurturing friendships—which, as it turns out, is something I want and need in my life—this information my body can offer me is becoming the vital guiding force I trust most.

What I am learning today is that trust comes over time, when you have a chance to see what the other person does with your heart, your stated needs and desires. If she is strong enough to be herself, she will be a solid presence to push against, but also leave you with a very clear sense that she wants you as you truly are and not some flimsy, people-pleasing copy. So each time you voice a limit or a desire, or ask for an audience, each time you communicate in attempts to reach for what you want, protest or connect, you come out of the interaction with a physical sense that you are safe, and that you matter, and knowing that you are desirable just as you are. This is what it's like to have healthy adult intimacy.

In Conclusion

As an Island, it takes some effort for me to commit to putting connection before my defenses against intimacy. I have tended to place a high value on achieving and accomplishing, appearing to have it all together. And in the labyrinth of my past marriages and raising children, I have spent a great deal of time disconnected from a sense of self-generated goals and dreams. I lived the first half of my life first doing what was expected of me, and later immersed in the trenches of carefully concealed crisis, dealing with the consequences of decisions I failed to make from a fully embodied, adult self.

I am willing to advocate for my body and avoid abandoning myself in the death trance of dissociation. Handing my power over to another, with a secret hope that they will attune to my unspoken needs is a relic of my childhood wounding. I am willing to step up to nourish a healthy sense of self, replacing my compulsion to attending to the needs of others first (my addiction to "saving" other people) and taking on their responsibilities with compassionate self-interest. My self-interest is a crucial part of the greater good and a necessary part of any authentic interaction with another.

Making the decision to heal developmental trauma necessarily means leaving the past behind you. This is not to say that what I have experienced wasn't important or that what came of it was not of immense importance. It just means that I now choose to show up as the fully functioning, embodied person I am, committed to the safety of the secure bond I have with myself. I hope to make embodiment so automatic that my default is no longer reacting to the emotional signals and needs of those I care about. In this new way of being, I have my own compass and I am a full and complete person.

Bringing the full embodied self to all our relationships is the one thing that is essential to attracting people who are safe and affirming into our lives; people with whom we can have mutuality, and with whom we are not required to be any way other than we are in order to be loved, accepted and cherished. Until I am unambiguously desirous of an exclusive relationship, I will experiment with connecting with others from the safety of my own intrapersonal couple bubble. Married first to myself, I can reap the benefits of interactions with healthy others and not-so-healthy others. I can use my body as it was intended; I can allow relationship with others to be calming and affirming to me—to be restorative. I can limit my contact with people who drain me or with whom I tend to disconnect from my own best interests. Married to myself, I can interact with people I have painful automatic patterns with and do what is necessary to remain embodied and on purpose in their presence. I can be authentic in the moment, checking in with myself when necessary, attuned enough to my own status that I know what I can and cannot afford to give, maintaining integrity with love, self-respect, balance, joy and pleasure in just the right measure.

FEELING THE BODY

"I was able to more permanently sense my body. Prior to that first session I knew I had a body but really could not sense it."

Robert was referred to me by a fellow therapist who worked from a more body-oriented perspective. Like many people today, Robert had been put on modern pharmaceuticals, including antibiotics, throughout his childhood and adolescence. He believes that the repeated doses of antibiotics that killed much of his healthy gut flora, led to the proliferation of pathogens, which ultimately produced negative psychotropic/psychoactive effects that, in combination with other factors in his life, profoundly impacted his physical, intellectual, academic, social, emotional, and spiritual experience of the world.

He went from having a gifted-level IQ as a second grader, with top-percentile performance in all academic areas, to effectively developing learning disabilities in multiple areas because his concentration and working memory became progressively worse throughout childhood and into his teenage years. Also during childhood, he developed unusual anxieties and obsessions that he still has difficulty describing or defining. The whole "antibiotic effect" culminated in a five-year prescription for tetracycline (for acne), and practically overnight, at age 15, he developed depression, anxiety, ADD and other hard-to-define, negative psychological phenomena so severe that he regularly thought about ending his life. He had no history of abuse, his parents were a solid unit (and loving/supportive), he lived in the same house since age three, was never bullied, and, in his own words, "Neither I nor my family had experienced any unusual psychosocial stressors of any kind."

As a teenager, the best explanation Robert could come up with for such a dramatic transformation was that his hormones were suddenly kicking in. "Puberty sucks," he told himself. For that reason, along with the fatigue, he looked upon this new state as a whole-body (and not just a mental or emotional) shift. As an avid tennis player, he knew what physical fatigue felt like—but this was something more fundamental. His soul felt fatigued.

Robert found himself in what he hoped would just be a life stage where he had virtually no capacity for pleasure. And he learned to accommodate by using common sense, and acting. His strategy involved getting past it with minimal suffering or long-term damage.

As he moved into adulthood, Robert continued to search for answers from professionals in the conventional medical arena. But because they were not able to help him, and in fact made things worse, Robert persevered, studying, asking questions, and working toward reclaiming his physical sensations and fully emotional self. When he found his way to my office, he had already gained a powerful ability to advocate for himself, and together we used a modified version of EMDR, following whatever sensory information we could find, and using bilateral stimulation through the use of vibrating tappers that he held, one in each hand. We continued our work together until I closed my private practice and moved south.

Robert continues to reclaim his integrated health and is now a psychotherapist, with a successful practice. What he experienced is an extreme example of dissociation from one's body and feelings, and it was caused not by emotional trauma, but attentive, responsible parents availing themselves of modern medicine to deal with common childhood illness. He describes the earliest stages of his physical integration as follows:

> *Specifically, the "tappers" we used during session vibrated one half of my body at a time—which then allowed me to sense it as whole. After my first couple of sessions, the effect wore off days later. But then, over time, it became more lasting and I was able to more permanently sense my body. Prior to that first session, I knew I had a body but really could not sense it (which in hindsight had been going on for a year or two). Since our first session, I've been slowly coming back from what I've been able to identify as the "dorsal vagal response," which is, essentially, the parasympathetic "shut-down" response to an overwhelming threat (external or internal). It's the only name I've found to describe how, emotionally, I still feel little else other than anxiety and irritability (though considerably less than I once did), and why I still don't feel hungry, feel full (after eating), or have a sex drive.*

As he continues to connect, incrementally, with his feelings,

Robert continues to be an advocate for his body, studying it and attending to it to meet its unique needs. He keeps me abreast of his progress and discoveries. Most recently he told me that he is functioning at about 95%.

My hypothesis is that the depression, ADD, and anxiety that I've experienced most of my life will be totally gone within 6 months; in some ways that are hard to explain, I'm already better than ever. If/when my hypothesis is proven correct, I will sing from the rooftops; it will be very, very difficult to shut me up.

Chapter 6 - The Body as a Bridge to The Self

The process of healing developmental trauma is a journey. It involves telling the story, learning about and accepting how the body works, developing a strong sense of self, and then bonding indelibly with it. And while all this might sound like some unattainable, pie-in-the-sky goal, we have at our disposal, if we are willing to use it, an ally that has been there all along: the body.

We cannot change our past, so we are charged with doing what we can, right now. We can 1) acknowledge that we have some catching up to do, 2) be willing to forgive ourselves for what might appear to be mistakes, or just plain inadequacy on our part, 3) be willing to consider the possibility that we really do deserve comfort, respect, protection, care and joy, 4) be willing to learn new skills, and 5) open our minds to different ways of experiencing the world.

Who am I? What do I like? How am I different from the people around me? These are very personal questions, and it is important that I, of all people, seek to find their answers.

Though we certainly don't want to swing too far in the direction of self-absorption or isolation, we need to spend *enough* time knowing what delights us. We cannot depend on someone else to do this for us, or hand the job over to someone who has stronger opinions. You undoubtedly have good reasons for being exactly where you are now. And from right where you are is a perfect place to begin the journey of knowing yourself.

This is where your body comes in. You will know what you like because just thinking of it will make you feel soft, relaxed, and light, not restricted, guarded, or confused. If you feel restricted, guarded or confused, stop and check out what's going on. If your body tells you that there is something going on that you don't like, pause and listen to it. Take responsibility for yourself and allow this information into your awareness. These are the signals that tell us to pause, reassess our own priorities, and take responsibility for choosing for ourselves. Deferring to the preferences of intimate others as a habit and ignoring unresolved differences and gray areas can quickly devolve into self-abandonment and its lazy sidekick, denial. It's okay to be flexible and generous, as long as that is your conscious choice, and you take the time to know yourself and what your preferences, goals and dreams actually are. This is not always easy, especially if it has not been your way. But its opposite represents disconnection from your body and ultimately from your self. When you remain disconnected from your own perspective, opinions, preferences and desires, you are not only abandoning yourself, but those around you as well, by not showing up as the whole person you are. If you are partnered, you are also abandoning your partner.

Through attunement with our bodies we are learning to read our own needs and desires and use them as resources for self-knowledge. We find out that what we want tells us something meaningful about ourselves. As Richo says in his book, *Daring to Trust*,

> *...we can practice a style that helps us know ourselves more deeply. We can first follow our need to see what it reveals about us and only after that seek fulfillment of the need, now understood more accurately. A need is then like the White Rabbit that leads Alice down the rabbit hole into Wonderland, the unconscious part of herself where she discovers qualities in herself previously unknown to her. A need can do that for us if instead of immediately running to someone for fulfillment, we take time to explore it. Perhaps our need for wholehearted unconditional love shows us what we missed in childhood.*[127]

Those of us who have disconnected from our feelings and learned to navigate life without the benefit of our felt emotions, have suspected that something is not right. But it's just a suspicion—a hunch. How can we know what "feeling" feels like? In the shutting down of our infant emotions, we concluded that it was too dangerous to feel. That conclusion, along with the decision to make it, remains hidden to us along with the unwanted feelings. All this supersedes everything until it is challenged, healed, and replaced.

In the same ways that we commit to staying connected with and loving and caring for ourselves and our bodies in a healthy and boundaried way, we create our relationships with intimate others. One is a reflection of the other. What I am proposing is that through a willingness to reconnect with our bodies, and to know and honor who we are, we can mend our ability to attach to others in healthy and rewarding ways as adults.

Along with not having a secure attachment with my parents, I was not encouraged to be uniquely me at home. The strategy I used to navigate this situation was to keep my self tightly contained, undeveloped, and unknown even to myself, and escape as soon as I could. I was not sure where I was going, but the urge to escape dominated my conscious and unconscious minds alike. So I arrived in the adult world not knowing what I lacked in terms of development, and had no idea what a self was. Attachment to myself was a foreign idea, and I had to patch it together, little by little. And that is what I've been doing ever since.

Take this quiz and see if it reflects how things have been going in your life:

T/F   I know how to listen to my emotions and appreciate their function in my life.
T/F   I appreciate the many things my body does for me every day.
T/F   What is good for my body is good for me.
T/F   It is safe to listen to my body.
T/F   I love my body.
T/F   I can name 20 things I appreciate about my body.
T/F   I enjoy my body.
T/F   My body's needs are reasonable.

Now go back and replace "my body" or "my emotions" with "my partner," "my relationship with my partner," or "my ex."

Studying intimacy through my relationship with my body, I am learning to be willing to listen to my bodily senses, trusting that it is safe to listen with an open heart. I am open to recognizing things I find attractive about my body. I push past taboos from my family legacy and discover that it's safe and appropriate to value and enjoy pleasure. I can modulate up—but I get to determine what I like (at some level of intensity, pleasure does become pain).

There are some in the mind-body field that argue that the body *is* the self. My body—if it *isn't* my self—at the very least informs me about my essence—who I am as a being uniquely me in the world. Trusting myself means that I trust my own body-mind as the most suitable instrument for living in a psychologically and spiritually healthy way.

Presence

It has not been an easy journey, this discarding of my defenses against intimacy. They are so automatic, and so slick. Behind a shield of busy-ness, and professional acumen, I can avoid vulnerable feelings; I can present a socially acceptable façade. And so this is why I am grateful, today, for the people throughout my life who have modeled being themselves, and communicated their personal experience with me at key points, when it might have been easier to process their experience alone. I will share one such experience of an interaction that brought home, and still characterizes, a deep internalization of my value that *relating and the relationship are more important than getting things done*. Not just that. When I think back on this story, I know that whatever the quality of my consciousness, I impact other people. I am *not* an island. I know, viscerally: Every. Single. Interaction. (with *every* other single living being) Counts.

Some years before I left the US for Mexico, I was deeply immersed in the personal vision of building and running a business, being a professional and using my skills and knowledge to support myself and my children. I was a warrior and it was a battle. I wore an armor of purpose which shielded my vision from anything the outside world might throw in my path to obstruct my success. I was single minded, determined, and very guarded. Everything was either about building myself as a professional and caring well for my children, or a distraction— something I needed to protect myself against. That is where my boundary was. I even placed my husband outside this unfortunate boundary.

But I was lucky enough during this time to cross paths with a particular person who was on a healing path not too different from mine. She caught me in my single-mindedness and gently called me on it, and I have never forgotten it. You see, inside my boundary, I felt safety and just enough belonging. But I needed to protect myself from anything outside. Outside of the very small circle that included me and my children, my sisters and a very small handful of friends, the shield I wore involved projecting a *mask* of caring and unconditional positive regard and safety. But the feeling was constant guardedness and the need to protect myself and my all-important time.

Carefully compartmentalized within my tiny circle and the proscribed bubble of my practice room with each of my clients, I engaged compassion mostly effortlessly (all this according to professional ethics, of course). But I had not yet figured out how to be safe, unguarded or compassionate in the world.

This person, who I'll identify as Diana Stelzer, had been injured in a car accident. I had an appointment with her, and she had asked me for a ride to the treatment she was giving me. We were trading sessions because her expertise was body-mind intuitive healing and I very much benefited from her work. I had previously paid top (absolutely deserved) rates for her services and felt newly thrilled and honored that she had proposed that we trade services at an equal exchange. On this particular day, I had gone to her studio for a session, and because her car had been totaled, she had asked me for a ride. In the role of "patient" I carefully guarded myself, enjoying the session, and then left, having a number of clients directly afterwards, and needing to stay aware of timing and preparation for those sessions. Diana's sessions had notoriously run past two hours, and I was feeling less than masterful in my ability to navigate that delicate balance of wanting all of Diana I could get and being able to transition gracefully from session to professional life. So without knowing it, I carried a sense of rigidity and defensiveness into the interaction.

The next time I saw Diana, she had something personal she needed to share with me. She described what had happened at that previous session and how it had struck her. I listened, and because I respect her deeply (and because she was able to tell me what she had on her mind with a good deal of skill and compassion), I was able to take in what she had to say. What I learned is that I had brought her to her office for my session and left her there with no consideration about how she was going to get back home. This had clearly caused her confusion—so much so that she had to work it and process it to figure out what had happened that made her feel unsettled, taken for granted, and bad.

What she helped me learn, at a very deep level, was that the potential for healing or harming another does not start and end according to clinical clock hours, but extends to include every moment in between, and every interaction with every living being I come into contact with. As Carl Jung famously said, "The meeting of two personalities is like the contact of two chemical substances: if there is any reaction, both are transformed." It took a while to realize it, but I was transformed that day.

As a person on this planet, every interaction with another sentient being is an opportunity to serve—not just the time between hours when I am on the clock in my chosen profession. Because Diana was willing to notice and honor what she felt, and share her experience with me, I have a better understanding about how I have been compulsive about work and protecting myself unnecessarily against the world. I better understand how rushing from one activity to the next without taking time to connect with myself or other people might be comfortable in that I maintain control, but at the expense of the quality of the interaction and the potential for experiencing something real and shared in the moment. I am still far from reaching mastery in this as a practice, but I better understand the value, to myself and those around me, of slowing down, examining how I feel, and honoring my interactions with others.

Healing trauma has the physical effect of helping someone to feel that the battle is actually over. Until this happens, we move through life physiologically braced, evaluative, and defensive. Compassion, according to Porges, "is 'neurophysiologically' incompatible with judgmental, evaluative, and defensive behaviors and feelings that recruit phylogenically older neural circuits regulating autonomic function."[128] He is engaged in research that actually gives us neurophysiological evidence that *physiological defensiveness turns off all the mammalian innovations of the autonomous nervous system—especially the "face-heart connection"*.

Compassion, he says, encompasses the newest branch of the ANS (the "Smart" or ventral vagus), and the judgmental, evaluative, and defensive behaviors would be represented by the sympathetic nervous system (SNS). When the SNS is imbalanced, stuck on, or dominant, it makes true compassion something that exists only in theory. Something we know we should feel, however physiologically unattainable. As Porges has put it, when someone breaks into your house with a gun, it doesn't make the most sense to attend to the needs of the baby. When we go into a defensive state, we physiologically recruit these older states. Shut-down behaviors would be understandable, he says, since our ancestors were turtles.[129] So whether we faint, go incoherently stupid, forget to breathe or blank out completely, we have our dorsal (or "Dumb") vagus nerve to thank. This is survival behavior. You will come back to the baby as soon as you come back to your senses.

DIVORCE—PARENTAL CONFLICT

"I'm two separate people. I'm not sure who I am."

Nasreen is the daughter of parents from two very different cultures. Her parents married when she was three months old, and divorced when she was eight.

Nasreen was almost one year old when she was brought to her father's country for the first time. Due to an emergency health situation of her father, her parents left her to be cared for by her father's family. Nasreen went from being breast fed and cared for full-time by her mother to being cared for by her paternal grandmother and her father's brother. Her diet changed abruptly to whatever food the family and their servants could get her to eat. Her uncle, who had never cared for a child, much less been in charge of diapering and comforting a baby, brought her back to her parents six weeks later by plane.

At the age of one year, a child does not have the ability to understand time, and could not have understood the words if someone had tried to explain to her that she would be reunited with her parents in a month or so. And for the first several days after they left her, she would wander from one room to another, searching for her parents. She eventually gave up on finding them, and the shock of abandonment was necessarily tucked away in the black box of her subconscious mind. The feelings, which she numbed out for the most part, would have likely included some combination of overwhelm, loneliness, abandonment and grief. And with the emotions separated from her awareness, she interacted with the world from a low-grade dissociative depression until she was reunited with her parents. This experience would set the foundation for Nasreen's ability to cope with later stressors, and feelings of abandonment and vulnerability.

When Nasreen was almost two, her parents moved to her father's country to live with his family, where her younger sister was born two years later. Both of her parents exhibited depressive symptoms at various times during the five years they lived there.

When Nasreen was seven, her mother took both children and fled the country, returning to her country of birth. Her father was extremely angry and felt humiliated by what his wife had done. One year later, he followed them in attempts to gain legal custody and bring the children back to his family. He did not believe that anything was more important than returning to his country with his children. The children, as stipulated by the court, shared time with both parents, alternating weekends and weeks between their homes.

So for the 18 months that their father lived in the same town as their mother, the children moved from the home of their father to the home of their mother and back again, each time needing to make that dreadful transition from melding, feeling, and understanding their father's perspective, to melding, feeling, and understanding their mother's perspective. This year and a half set the tone for the remainder of their childhood, where they would live in two very different worlds with two equally compelling stories, two very different sets of facts, and two very different emotional environments—both of which were valid and understandable at some level.

As the weeks and months went by, and Nasreen continued to see the suffering that her father was experiencing, she sensed a dilemma. She loved and cared about her father. But the contempt with which he talked about her mother settled heavily on her shoulders, and she didn't like how it felt. "Your mother ruined my life," he would say, almost daily.

Nasreen was one who learned early on how to read people, and she had a special gift for getting what she wanted if she put her mind to it. One day she decided to tell her father that she didn't like it when he spoke such things of her mother. His response was to assume the role of the victim. "What?!" he said. "Are you seriously going to take her side after everything she's done to me?" He sulked for a while, intermittently withdrawn, and furious. He would refuse to make eye contact, using a technique he was known to refer to as "the silent treatment," to make sure she knew he was serious. "If you love your mother so much," he finally said, "why don't you just go live with her." His response quickly taught her that this was unacceptable territory. She would be more careful next time to keep her feelings to herself. Ultimately, in order to protect him, she would put his needs and feelings first.

Nasreen had no way of knowing or understanding the developmental implications of what was happening. When her father spoke disparaging or hateful words about her mother, she took his words into herself. So everything that he said to her about her mother embedded itself deep within her psyche. And the lesson reinforced what she had already learned about emotions: they were dangerous. This incident among many with her father taught her that her emotions could hurt other people.

Moving back and forth from the home of her mother to the home of her father under these circumstances was not easy for Nasreen, and she knew that telling her mother about her father's behavior would be a further betrayal to him, and she could not, under any circumstances, hurt her father more, as he was clearly suffering because of what her mother had done. While the girls were with their father he instructed them to do mean things to their mother as a means for camaraderie and revenge. He would ask, "Do you have any good news?" When they had something to report, he would laugh and laugh.

Understand, now, that at this age, developmentally, children are not capable of distinguishing themselves emotionally from their parents. They are not yet individuated, and they naturally meld and blend with the adult they are physically nearest, in the present moment. This is a means of safety, and ultimately survival.

Nasreen learned to be very good at separating her father's world from her mother's world. The information she held in separate parts of her mind she carefully guarded, lest she hurt or betray someone she loved. She learned the meaning of the phrase, "take it to your grave," very early on, because she strived to be a person of great integrity.

Finally, after none of his attempts to legally demonstrate that their mother was unfit or incapable of keeping the children safe, Nasreen's father gave up. Neither of the girls wanted to see him "lose" this battle, and in many ways they felt that they had let him down when he finally gave up in despair.

With the development of her superego, Nasreen internalized her father's rules, which fledged into the voice of her very own, full-blown, trauma-inducing inner critic. Not knowing any different, Nasreen continued to do what she could to cover up the state of affairs in her head. This process required energy and attention, as the shamefulness and contempt she had internalized from her father, and the other "parts" that emerged to offset her resulting vulnerability, were programs always running underneath what she shared with the outside world. Through this set of circumstances, Nasreen learned to always think before talking. She learned that to ensure her safety, and that of her sister, she would need to calculate the potential effects of any verbal or non-verbal (facial) expression or response before sharing it.

As an adult, Nasreen currently describes herself, in the emotional realm, as someone who is slow to react. A significant period of time needs to pass for her to know how she feels about unfamiliar events, and interactions with new people.

She notices that needing anything from others can feel especially dangerous. As she learned early on, it is not safe or prudent to seek support or understanding from others (that it can actually cause them pain).

Fragmentation into "parts" is a way children cope when faced with extreme pressure, and it is also a form of dissociation. While Nasreen appeared to function and behave like other healthy, normal children, underneath, she carefully guarded any feelings of vulnerability, weakness, or dependency. Appearing to have everything neatly "together," the various parts of her psyche remained dissociated from one another, her emotional feelings dissociated from her conscious awareness, and her internal chaos dissociated from a very "together" exterior.

Six Stories of Dissociation

When all is said and done, dissociation is a disconnect between things or functions that were designed to be connected. Our case stories depict some of the ways dissociation can appear as a result of trauma. In the following section I briefly recap the stories and then list the tools that each individual uses to overcome the effects of trauma.

Chapter	Individual Example	Type of Dissociation
Chapter 1: Trauma	Tracy	Fragmentation of Self
Chapter 2: Dissociation	Mel	Depersonalization
Chapter 3: Parenting	Toni	Emotional Flashback
Chapter 4: Body	Lu	Structural Separation
Chapter 5: Adult Intimacy	Robert	Structural Separation
Chapter 6: Bridge to Self	Nasreen	Fragmentation of Self

Tracy was selected by her family to play the role of scapegoat. As such, she learned that a worthwhile life necessarily characterized sacrifice and abuse, and that no sacrifice was too big if the cause was worthy. Her go-to tools are:

- Actively reconstructing the story, with the help of relatives or family friends if necessary.
- Using recent/adult problems and patterns to help piece together a more complete understanding of the dynamics from childhood that she had blocked from her awareness.

- Using current/adult problems and patterns to help identify beliefs she picked up from her childhood that no longer serve her.
- Learning to recognize and disallow self-abuse.
- Spiritual practices.

Mel was born with a genetic mutation that resulted in the need to be medically monitored and undergo invasive and painful medical procedures from the time she was one until she underwent corrective surgery at the age of seven. Her go-to tools are:

- Recognizing the strengths and abilities that developed as a result of the adversity she faced.
- Recognizing the development of unique and valuable character traits that resulted from what happened.
- Using intellect and research to gain knowledge.
- Creating a safe place in the imagination.
- Engaging curiosity to understand younger versions of her self.
- Interpreting the body's signals as a call to make necessary changes.

Toni did not bond securely with her parents. Because of interruptions in attunement and insufficient repairs beginning in infancy and continuing through childhood, she did not develop a felt sense of safety with her caretakers. She also grew up watching her older sister being scapegoated and abused. As a result of both these factors she failed to form a strong sense of self or differentiate from her parents when she was a teenager. Her go-to tools are:

- Ego strengthening, development of self in adulthood.

192

- Engaging curiosity with younger versions of her self.
- Using intellect and research to gain information and knowledge.
- Reaching out to find ways to be seen and accepted.
- Joy and pleasure in just the right measure.

Lu's mother was very ill when she was born, and eventually left the home when Lu was three. Lu also experienced sexual abuse by a close relative. Her adult relationships have been characterized by intensity. Her go-to tools are:

- Learning the body's language.
- Bodywork targeting pain and tension.
- Creating a safe place in the imagination.
- Using bodily sensations to guide psychotherapy.
- Using the parenting experience as an opportunity to learn and grow.
- Using textures, colors and nature to stay grounded.
- Development of emotional boundaries.
- Interpreting the body's signals as a call to make necessary changes.
- Use of boundaries to prevent abuse (from inside or outside).

Robert's dissociation was caused by modern pharmaceuticals, which altered the naturally protective microbiome in his gut. Arguably, some early relational trauma could have been at play, but this account focuses on the physical etiology of his condition. His go-tools are:

- Self-advocacy.
- Visualizing a desired future with clarity and fully

embodied emotional response.

- Bodywork.
- Using bodily sensations to guide psychotherapy.
- Bilateral stimulation (modified EMDR).
- Using intellect and research to gain information and knowledge.

Nasreen developed an ability to function in the two violently opposing worlds of her warring parents by fragmenting into multiple selves that were quite separate from one another. Her history of "forgotten" trauma, which she kept safely guarded in the "black box," helped to shape the ways she would later respond to stress. Her go-to tools include:

- Allowing herself to know the story, with the help of relatives or family friends.
- Recognizing the strengths and abilities that developed as a result of the adversity she faced.
- Recognizing the development of unique and valuable character traits that resulted from what happened.
- Using the raising of her own daughter to help her connect with her inner resources and make conscious choices that serve them both.

Tools Necessary for Overcoming the Effects of Trauma

Here are thirteen tools that you can consider carrying in your own toolbox.

1 - Slow Down. Take your time. Take all the time you need. If something feels peculiar, or not quite right, pause. Breathe. This is not a battle. For most of us, it's not even a crisis. Chances are, it's okay to relax and be where you are instead of rushing to the next thing.

2 - Engage curiosity. Take the time to recognize the repeating patterns in your life and be open to how they can help you understand the perspective of your younger self. Use them to help you piece together a better understanding of the dynamics from childhood that you don't consciously remember. Studying these patterns can also help you identify beliefs you inadvertently picked up along the way that no longer serve you.

3 - Tell your story. Actively reconstruct the story. Enlist the help of a therapist, relatives or a family friend if necessary. Whether you get therapy or not, know that telling your story— at the very minimum to yourself, but to at least one safe other if that is possible—is profoundly important. Wallin says that putting experience into words is a part of how we integrate it.

> *...when we lack words for our experience, our experience tends to be much more gripping, much more overwhelming. I think having words is a way to communicate about our experience, so that putting hitherto unverbalized experience into words allows us to feel less alone with it. And feeling less alone helps us to feel less overwhelmed.*[130]

4 - Recognize and appreciate what is right and good.
The three tools above make it more possible to use this one: recognizing the unique and valuable character traits, strengths and abilities that developed as a result of the adversity you faced. Without using this tool, you may never truly understand the things that make you uniquely *you*.

Moving this tool so that it is outward facing, you can scan your life and recognize how what you are longing for is already true. Your desires already have been, or will be, fulfilled in ways you might have overlooked. Be flexible and allow these good things to come to you. Instead of expecting the people and things around you to be any different than they are, increase your ability to approve of them just as they are. Use your keen sensitivity to spot and appreciate the greatness of others, the skills that abound all around you, the resourcefulness, the intelligence, the courage to take a chance and possibly fail. Open your eyes to what life is bringing you in this moment. Look for ways the people around you are sharing themselves with you and showing you that you matter.

5 - Engage imagination. Use your imagination to calm you when you are overwhelmed, or to help you usher in a new experience for yourself. Let yourself imagine what once calmed and soothed you and allow it to calm and soothe you once more. Understand that your creative mind cannot distinguish between something vividly imagined and something actually experienced. Spend time imagining in detail the things you most desire, along with your whole-hearted emotional response in some unspecified future time when you fully receive them. You can also use this practice to identify and address any blocks you may have erected against receiving your heart's desires.

6 - Rewire the brain. Good therapy is often necessary to identify and address the effects of early relational trauma. But effective trauma therapy will effectively rewire the brain, whether it is through the resonance created in the therapeutic relationship, the integration of left and right hemispheres, the use of somatic therapies, or the building of synaptic bridges between our powerless child selves and our adult resources. Here is what Richo says:

> Past experiences of violated trust leave post-traumatic scars. In the present, what hampers us is not our experience of trust itself but our freeze reaction to it. Time stands still, and the past interrupts and usurps the present. Trauma therapy shows how our body can be a resource in dealing with our stress reaction stemming from abuse in early life. This happens not by minimizing the facts but by redesigning our relationship to them. We cannot rewrite our story, but we can rewire our brain. This happens when our memories remain intact but without the emotional charge that can cause ongoing damage to our capacity to trust.[131]

7 - Develop a healthy sense of self. In building a sense of self that is increasingly known to you, you bring to any relationship a durable "I matter." This will allow you to advocate for yourself when you meet resistance. This takes effort, and it goes hand-in-hand with the following tool: developing healthy boundaries. We cannot be deeply respected or even known by anyone else unless we know who we are. Let your emotions and needs inform you in this regard and show up in relationships with all your needs, preferences, goals, aspirations and feelings. Be the gift that you are and share yourself in your greatness. Everyone benefits when you show up as the whole, one-of-a-kind person you are.

8 - Develop healthy boundaries. Emotional boundaries give us a way to separate our emotional experience from the emotional experience of others. The three tools for building boundaries that I offer in *Boundaries 101* are 1) *Strengthening the ability to tolerate unpleasant emotions*, 2) *Building in a pause before responding to the requests of others, and* 3) *Asking for clarification.* [132]

When we reach adulthood without feeling safe in our bodies, rather than experiencing our own emotions, we have learned to habitually project our attention outward. Calling ourselves empaths, we have learned to "feel" the feelings of others instead of our own. And some of us are very good at this. Learning to shift our focus to the bedrock of our own emotional experience (through attention to the body) is necessary for us, and yes, it can be difficult at first. But it allows us to experience healthy adult interaction, where we stay anchored in our own experience in the moment. Then, when we encounter spoken or unspoken emotional impressions from others, we have the ability to distinguish between what is ours and what is not. We can count on our own emotional intelligence to inform us when *we* have pending needs, priorities or concerns that should rightly be addressed first.

9 - Strengthen the ability to tolerate emotions. Once we have begun the important work of separating our emotions from those of the people around us, the task of experiencing our own emotions, past and present becomes much more feasible. Doing our emotional work enables us to both develop our boundaries and tolerate the intensity of emotions, and with these tools we can more predictably live in the present, feeling and using our emotions as they come up, rather than habitually blocking and avoiding them. Strengthening the ability to tolerate emotions increases one's ability to control impulses, to feel a feeling without having to act on it, or act it out. As a way of moving through life, it also opens the way for sharing who we really are, and being alive and aware in the present moment, rather than regressing and operating on automatic pilot. Your emotional work might also include strengthening your ability to tolerate safety, comfort, support, and pleasure, and identifying the ways you have valued being right or being in control over being happy.

10 - Leave your expectations at the door. Be open to experiencing something different. If you already know what's going to happen, or if you have an attachment to a specific outcome, you will bring rigidity to your relationships and rigidity will be reflected back.

11 - Make friends with your body. If your body is trying to tell you something, pause, and ask for clarification. It will tell you what it needs. Attend to the subtler messages; don't wait until it's screaming at you to give it your time and attention. Earn the trust of your vulnerable, corporeal self through listening to the information that your body provides. It will make all the difference in the world when you are relating with the people and circumstances around you. Adopting a discipline may help you develop this relationship with your body. Yoga, meditation, tai chi, chi kung, tantra, chanting, breathwork and attuned nutrition can all help you forge this mutual relationship. Invest the time to find out what type of nutrition your body needs to thrive, as there is no one diet that fits all. At the very least, give some consideration to the quality of the food you nourish your body with,[133] and reduce your toxin exposure[134] to the extent possible. It may take some time, but as you begin to trust the information you receive from your body, also reconnect with your instincts and intuition. And so you become a better judge of other people and complicated situations as they arise. Though we can't expect ourselves to be automatically fluent in the language of our bodies, it is no longer acceptable to ignore, discount, or minimize the messages we receive from our corporeal selves.

12 - Practice basic kindness. We naturally desire physical and emotional closeness. Richo says that closeness happens "through engaging with one another and responding to one another" through showing the five A's, which are attention, acceptance, appreciation, affection, and allowing.[135] Use these five A's as a discipline to connect reliably with yourself. Nurture a trusted relationship with yourself by giving these five things to and receiving them from yourself. Once you have gained some trust and mastery within yourself, you will more likely be able to experience physical and emotional closeness with others.

13 - Continue to learn and grow. Use your intellect. Research and find out what others are discovering that helps to shed light on this complex topic. Whether your interest is neurobiology, the connection between attachment and adult intimacy, the connection between the gut and mental health, effective therapy and quantum physics or child development, the broad inclusiveness of what "normal" actually *is* in the scope of human evolution, or anything else—learning promotes growth, provides you with mentors and role models and is an invaluable tool to include in your box. Enjoy it!

Here is my commitment to myself today: I am willing to continue my work toward being able to maintain a connection with my own feelings while attuning to the feelings of others. I am willing to stay untriggered because living in the here and now is where my greatest potential truly lies. I am willing to forego perfectionism as I navigate my life, learning to use the information that is available to me, always, from my body to determine my truth from moment to moment. Today, choosing and doing, on purpose, what I came here to do, involves using the skills and tools that have developed as a result of my life experience to engage life fully, staying connected to my joy and pleasure in just the right measure through the information that is always available to me as my fully embodied felt sense. I am willing to speak up, to be who I am, moment by moment, to stay connected to myself no matter what. And from here, I can be of best service to the world and those I love.

And so I come back to this: In order to maintain a healthy balance with an intimate other, one must be committed to embodiment. We must be willing to be in mutual partnership with the body, accepting its input for fully informed decisions that are uniquely ours. We must love, accept and cherish our selves with all our parts, no matter what state of fragmentation or integration. And to stay on the path of embodiment, one must commit to returning to the self as many times as it takes while these skills are learned and mastered.

Appendix I
Emotions: Messengers of Truth

Sadness and Grief can feel like heaviness in the body, like pressure on the chest. They can bring tears with or without a feeling of sadness. They can also be tearless. They can show up in the form of heavy sighing throughout the day, according to Karla McLaren, or a physical sensation of winding or meandering. The function of sadness is to signal us to slow down, take some time to regroup, rest and assess our losses. The physical benefit of sadness and grief is release. Until and unless you recognize and acknowledge your sadness and grief, you are holding tightly onto something from the past, which obstructs entry for new and good things into your life. Sadness, once you understand it, marks the end of a chapter, which always means the beginning of a new (and better) one. It is surprising how often the intensity of sadness and grief transforms into a deep, deep sensation of love and compassion.

Anger, Annoyance, Resentment, Rage. People who don't cop to being angry (probably because anger was not allowed for them when they were growing up) will tell me "I'm not an angry person." They feel annoyed, they say they feel bothered or fed up. They tell me they feel confused because what other people are telling them doesn't line up with what they are doing. As long as they remain in denial about what they know (that they really *don't like* what others around them are doing), they will have trouble moving past that hump of annoyance and into righteous indignation. Once they're able to feel that, it's not too difficult to feel the anger, which I'll talk about in a minute. But first I want to tell you about rage. People tend to get confused about anger—mistakenly believing that rage is anger. Actually, rage is not an emotion, but a behavior. It is terror and lack of boundaries. People who have experienced the rage of their parents or spouses often vow never to do that to anyone else. They thus incorrectly conclude that it is not responsible to be angry. And they are rightfully frightened of someone who is in their physical proximity who is making a lot of noise and threatening to explode. *That*, the person decides, *is not something I want to feel. Ever. It's way too scary. Someone is going to get hurt.* But anger is something different entirely. Anger is not an overwhelming emotion. It is a firm clarity. A sense of knowing, when one cuts through the bullshit denial, other people's confusion and projections, and abuse. In therapy, anger rarely even shows up for more than a few seconds, a fiery spark or sometimes a resistance to even entering the emotional realm. Once they're past that, it's obvious how "anger" was a shield the individual was using to protect his or her soft underbelly emotions like vulnerability, loneliness, grief, abandonment, embarrassment, shame, inadequacy.

Healthy anger is the byproduct of a successful therapy session because emerging healthy anger is simply a known and felt boundary. It's strength, clarity, a knowingness of what is true for oneself (that is different from the other) and a fearlessness about communicating one's limits to others who might not really want to hear about them. It is actually a private emotion, signaling the person that something isn't right, and that it is time to make adjustments (usually interpersonal) to reinstate or create feelings of safety and comfort where these had been compromised before. With the boundary emerges the budding of the vulnerable but protected, supported self.

Another idea I recently came across is that "pleasers" are very angry people. People who spend their time and energy trying to please others without learning what they *themselves* want, or pursuing their own desires, have a chronic undercurrent of unmet needs, and a feeling of resentment about this situation (When will it be *my* turn?), though they are usually unaware of their resentment, disappointment, and frustration, and have no idea how to turn the situation around. In such people, the feeling of resentment is still the red flag that something is out of balance. Changes are called for, though cutting through all the patterns, attitudes and beliefs in order to actually change "pleasing" behavior is no small feat. Thus, pleasers very often go through life unaware of their anger, but remain convinced of their selfless virtue. They come across as self righteous, angry and judgmental of the "non-pleasers" around them, who to them seem to have undeserved freedoms and rights.

Shame is another emotion that people often don't think much about until they enter therapy. Karla McLaren says it's anger turned inward. It helps us make sure we are behaving with others in a correct and honorable manner. It can be a slippery, sneaky emotion because it doesn't seem to have a clearly recognizable sensation. More often, it just seems like this thick or sticky muck or darkness surrounding an issue. Once you know what to look for, it is obvious that you are dealing with shame, and you can assess whether or not you want to make adjustments to your behavior with others in order to stay in integrity with yourself and your values. It is good to visit and revisit your healthy shame, as it is what helps us interact with others in social and responsible ways. But shame can be a crippling emotion among people who were often controlled with various forms of violence (including shame and coercion) as children. Parents who were shamed as children often use this technique with their children because it can get them short-term results, when they don't have healthier parenting skills. These parents shame their children for any behavior they want to discourage, which results in over-active guilt that can linger for a lifetime and color a person's entire worldview until it is addressed. I find that shame, once it is recognized and named and described, is completely manageable. It's when you aren't aware of it that it can do so much damage.

Appendix II
Complex Post Traumatic Stress Disorder
(Excerpts from Pete Walker)

CPTSD is a more severe form of post-traumatic stress disorder. It is differentiated from this better-known trauma syndrome by five of its most common and troublesome features: emotional flashbacks, toxic shame, self-abandonment, a vicious inner critic and social anxiety.

Emotional flashbacks are perhaps the most noticeable and characteristic feature of CPTSD. Survivors of traumatizing abandonment are extremely susceptible to painful emotional flashbacks, which unlike PTSD do not typically have a visual component.

Trauma occurs when attack or abandonment triggers a fight/flight response so intensely that the person cannot turn it off once the threat is over. He becomes stuck in an adrenalized state. His sympathetic nervous system is locked "on" and he cannot toggle into the relaxation function of the parasympathetic nervous system.

Characteristics that signal CPTSD include a diminishment or absence of:

Self-acceptance
Clear sense of identity
Self-compassion
Self-protection
Capacity to draw comfort from relationship
Ability to relax
Capacity for full self-expression
Willpower and motivation
Peace of mind
Self-care

Belief that life is a gift
Self-esteem
Self-confidence

13 Steps for Managing Emotional Flashbacks

(Focus on <u>Underlined portion</u> when flashback is active.)

1. <u>Say to yourself: "I am having a flashback."</u> Flashbacks take you into a timeless part of your psyche that feels as helpless, hopeless and surrounded by danger as you were in childhood. The feelings and sensations you are experiencing are past memories that cannot hurt you now.

2. <u>Remind yourself: "I feel afraid but I am not in danger!"</u> I am safe now, here in the present." Remember you are now in the safety of the present, far from the danger of the past.

3. <u>Own your right/need to have boundaries.</u> Remind yourself that you do not have to allow anyone to mistreat you, you are free to leave dangerous situations and protest unfair behavior.

4. <u>Speak reassuringly to the Inner child.</u> The child needs to know that you love her/him unconditionally—that she/he can come to you for comfort and protection when she/he feels lost and scared.

5. <u>Deconstruct eternity thinking.</u> In childhood, fear and abandonment felt endless—a safer future was

unimaginable. Remember this flashback will pass as it always has before.

6. <u>Remind yourself that you are in an adult body,</u> with allies, skills and resources to protect you that you never had as a child. (Feeling small and fragile is a sign of a flashback.)

7. <u>Ease back into your body</u>. Fear launces you into "heady" worrying, or numbing and spacing out.

   1. <u>Gently ask your body to relax</u>. Feel each of your major muscle groups and softly encourage them to relax. (Tightened muscles send false danger signals to your brain).

   2. <u>Breathe deeply and slowly</u>. (Holding your breath also signals danger).

   3. <u>Slow Down</u>. Rushing presses your brain's flight response button.

   4. <u>Find a safe place</u> to unwind and soothe yourself: wrap yourself in a blanket, hold a pillow or a stuffed animal, lie down on your bed or in a closet or in a bath; take a nap.

   5. <u>Feel the fear in your body without reacting to it.</u> Fear is just an energy in your body. It cannot hurt you if you do not run from it.

8. <u>Resist the Inner Critic's Drasticizing and Catastrophizing</u>.

   1. <u>Use thought stopping</u> to halt the critic's endless exaggerations of danger, and its constant planning to control the uncontrollable. Channel the anger

of self-attack into saying "NO" to your critic's unfair self-criticism.

2. Use thought substitution and thought correction to replace negative thinking with a memorized list of your qualities and accomplishments.

9. Allow yourself to grieve. Flashbacks are opportunities to release old, unexpressed feelings of fear, hurt and abandonment. Validate and soothe your child's past experience of helplessness and hopelessness. Healthy grieving can turn your tears into self-compassion and your anger into self-protection.

10. Cultivate safe relationships and seek support. Take time alone when you need it, but don't let shame isolate you. Feeling shame doesn't mean you are shameful. Educate your intimates about flashbacks and ask them to help you talk and feel your way through them.

11. Learn to identify the types of triggers that lead to flashbacks. Avoid unsafe people, places, activities and triggering mental processes. Practice preventive maintenance with these steps when triggering situations are unavoidable.

12. Figure out what you are flashing back to. Flashbacks are opportunities to discover, validate and heal your wounds from past abuse and abandonment. They also point to your still unmet developmental needs and can provide you with motivation to get them met.

13. <u>Be patient with a slow recovery process</u>. It takes time in the present to become de-adrenalized, and considerable time in the future to gradually decrease the intensity, duration and frequency of flashbacks. Real recovery is a gradually progressive process (often two steps forward, one step back), not an attained salvation fantasy. Don't beat yourself up for having a flashback.

Walker, Pete. *CPTSD Surviving to Thriving: A Guide and Map for Recovering from Childhood Trauma*, 2014. http://www.pete-walker.com/ Used with permission of the author.

Appendix III
Prompts for Developing a Stronger Sense of Self
Quotes from Eva Pierrakos
(*The Pathwork of Self-Transformation*)

"Clarifying beliefs; clarifying convictions; clarifying values; clarifying priorities; formulating life plans; formulating life goals; staying responsibly connected to persons on my own family tree; defining the 'I' in key relationships; addressing important emotional issues as they arise."

"Reconnecting and defining where we stand on important relationship issues, but in a new way that is focused on the self, not the other."

"I need to focus on what I want to say 'about the self' and 'for the self.'"

"Separateness refers to the preservation of the 'I' within the 'we'—the ability to acknowledge and respect differences and to achieve authenticity within the context of connectedness."

"We cannot navigate clearly within a relationship unless we can live without it. [We therefore need to be working toward] formulating a life plan that neither requires nor excludes marriage [,] planning for our own economic future and formulating long-range work and career goals. Yet such planning—which requires both personal and social change—not only ensures the well-being of the self but also puts us on more solid ground for negotiating relationships with intimate others."

Eva Pierrakos, *The Pathwork of Self-Transformation*. New York: Bantam Books, 1990.

Appendix IV
Weinholds' Development Chart

Stage of Development and Primary Task

Co-Dependency (Conception to Six Months) **Bonding and Attachment**

- *Essential Developmental Processes of Individual Evolution*
  - **Mother:**
    - Mother receives good prenatal care and support
  - **Child:**
    - experiences a non-violent birth with immediate interventions to heal any birth trauma
    - achieves consistent, secure bonding and attachment with mother and/or other adult care-givers
    - learns primal trust in parents through a consistent resonant connection
    - learns emotional resiliency skills
    - creates a secure internal working model of self/other
    - learns healthy emotional communication and social engagement skills with parents and others
    - bonds securely with siblings and extended family
- *Suggested Experiences for Completing The Essential Developmental Processes of Individual Evolution*
  - **Mother:**
    - maintains a high-quality diet and reduces environmental stressors to prevent the risk of cortisol production during pregnancy
    - receives effective postnatal emotional and physical support
    - provides nurturing, respectful touch and eye contact; she gazes at, sings to, and speaks to the child in loving ways
  - **Parents:**
    - plan for and want the child

- build prenatal relationship with the child
- use nonviolent birthing practices
- nurse and room-in at the hospital and have prolonged skin-to-skin contact between child and each parent in the first 12-24 hours following birth
  - **Child:**
    - gets timely emotional and tactile comforting to help heal developmental traumas caused by disruptions in resonant connection to parents
    - receives unconditional love from parents
    - receives authentic mirroring and validation of his or her essence from parents
  - **Immediate and extended family members:**
    - provide consistent, nurturing, and empathic contact
    - provide comfortable and protective environment to meet the child's needs for safety and survival

Stage of Development and Primary Task
Counter-Dependency (Six to Thirty-six Months) **Separation and Individuation**
- *Essential Developmental Processes of Individual Evolution*
  - **Child:**
    - completes the psychological separation process with parents
    - learns to safely explore his or her environment
    - learns to trust and regulate his or her own thoughts, feelings, and behaviors in socially appropriate ways
    - internalizes appropriate physical and social limits
    - develops healthy narcissism
    - resolves internal conflicts between oneness and separateness (I'm okay, you're okay)
    - bonds with self
    - continues to build secure internal working model
    - completes his or her individuation or psychological birth process
- *Suggested Experiences for Completing The Essential Developmental Processes of Individual Evolution*

- **Parents:**
  - offer timely help in healing any narcissistic wounds or developmental traumas that interfere with resonance
  - give the child permission and support to safely explore his or her environment; they give the child twice as many yeses as nos during this time
  - rearrange environment to provide safety
  - understand and respect the child's need to develop internal regulation of emotions, especially shame
  - help the child identify self-needs, as opposed to the needs of others
  - model how to directly ask to have one's needs met
  - use nonshaming responses in limit-setting and discipline
  - give positive support for the child's efforts to develop an autonomous Self
- **Adult Caregivers:**
  - help the child quickly reestablish the resonant connection with the mother when it's disrupted
  - offer empathy and compassion as the child learns to regulate his or her conflicting emotions, thoughts, and behaviors
  - offer authentic mirroring and validation of the child's essence
  - offer permission for the child to be a separate individual and to trust his or her internal impulses

Stage of Development and Primary Task

Independence (Three to Six Years) **Mastery of Self and Environment**

- *Essential Developmental Processes of Individual Evolution*
  - **Child:**
    - learns to cooperate with others
    - learns to negotiate with others to get his or her needs met
    - learns to accept responsibility for his or her personal behaviors and life experiences
    - experiences secure bonding with peers and other adults
    - develops a social conscience
    - bonds securely with his or her culture
    - bonds securely with the planet
    - lives his or her life as an authentic adult
    - bonds securely with own children
    - understands the influence of incomplete developmental processes on his or her life and how to successfully heal developmental traumas
- *Suggested Experiences for Completing The Essential Developmental Processes of Individual Evolution*
  - **Parents:**
    - rearrange home environment to support the child's mastery of self-care (eating, dressing, and toilet training)
    - support the child's development of effective internal limits and consequences
    - help the child learn appropriate emotional self-regulation and control
    - help the child learn to trust his or her inner sense of wisdom and guidance
    - provide the child with experiences for the safe exploration of nature

- help the child develop sensory relationships with nature
- provide for reciprocal social interactions with other children
- teach cross-relational thinking, including empathy and respect for others
- help the child develop cause/effect problem-solving skills
- **Immediate and extended family members:** offer nurturing, supportive, and consistent contact
- **Adults** model partnership solutions to conflicts

Stage of Development and Primary Task
Interdependence *(Six to Twenty-nine Years)* **Cooperation and Negotiation Skills**
- *Essential Developmental Processes of Individual Evolution*
  - **Child:**
    - learns to cooperate with others
    - learns to negotiate with others to get his or her needs met
    - learns to accept responsibility for his or her personal behaviors and life experiences
    - experiences secure bonding with peers and other adults
    - develops a social conscience
    - bonds securely with his or her culture
    - bonds securely with the planet
    - lives his or her life as an authentic adult
    - bonds securely with own children
    - understands the influence of incomplete developmental processes on his or her life and how to successfully heal developmental traumas
- *Suggested Experiences for Completing The Essential Developmental Processes of Individual Evolution*
  - **Parents:**
    - model effective cooperative social engagement skills in couple, family, and peer relationships

- **Child:**
  - seeks to learn negotiation skills to get his or her needs met in healthy ways
  - seeks solutions to his or her conflicts that honor the needs of all parties involved
  - seeks adult validation of the importance of keeping his or her relationship agreements
  - seeks an adult model that can teach him or her empathy and compassion for others
  - seeks adults who can teach him or her intuitive language and thinking skills
  - seeks nurturing, supportive, and consistent contact from immediate and extended family members
  - seeks support from parents and other adults on how to build sustainable relationships with other adults and how to find a primary love partner
  - seeks adult input on the values of his or her cultural group and how to overcome any limits imposed by family and culture
  - seeks personal meaning and a personal mission within the context of the "global family"
  - seeks information and skills for healing his or her developmental traumas
  - seeks assistance in developing systemic and transsystemic thinking

  - **Adults** encourage the development of an internalized "safety parent" allowing safe risk-taking behaviors

Weinhold, Barry K. & Janae B. *Healing Developmental Trauma: A Systems Approach to Counseling Individuals, Couples & Families.* Denver: Love Publishing, 2010 (102-104).
Used with permission of the authors.

Appendix V
Advanced Intimacy Affirmations
(Pointing at the moon.)

- I am consistently able to connect with and use my body to inform my direction, my course.
- I am consistently able to connect with the value that for me, personally, connecting is more important than accomplishing and that in reality, all is *already* accomplished.
- I am consistently able to connect with my ability to play and value the pleasure of connecting over accomplishment.
- I consistently choose being happy over being right.
- I consistently choose being happy over being in control.
- I am consistently able to choose a rich, full, authentic life alongside others who are having their own experiences.
- I am consistently able to stay connected with myself when I am with intimate others.
- I approach my intimate relationships with humility, honesty, openness and trust.
- I am consistently able to recognize fear when it crops up as judgment, blame or criticism, and to filter it carefully.
- I appreciate my critical voice because it has served an important role in the past—to protect me from intimacy.
- Today I am softer. I am powerful, but I allow myself to be adored and loved and supported without fear.

Appendix VI
What to Expect from Attachment-Focused EMDR

So in explaining how EMDR works, we can think about trauma as experiences that have happened to us, that haven't had a chance to fully process. Unlike regular memories, which are filed away in the brain in their proper places, allowing us to use what we have learned, and cast off information that isn't particularly useful or necessary to our survival, trauma is handled differently in our systems. When something happens that overwhelms our circuitry (we believe our basic safety or survival is threatened in some way, the emotions are just too much), this can be classified as trauma. With a trauma, the body adaptively responds by compartmentalizing this memory (all the sensory information), or storing it in a form that is still unprocessed.

An unprocessed memory still contains all the parts: smells, tastes, images, sounds, body sensations, beliefs—as if the incident just happened, or is still happening. And this memory is stored away in that "compartment" or box, so that we can concentrate on our daily responsibilities. If it were not suppressed, or compartmentalized, it would likely be too distracting for us to function.

These compartments are great in that we owe our survival to them. But over the long run, we notice that in moments when we are tired or hungry, or something happens that is somehow similar to that original event, the compartment or the box begins to leak, and we feel the same way we did during the original incident, or we behave the way we did when we were, say, 6—when the trauma happened, or something irrational pops into our heads (this is because our 6-year-old thought or our 6-year-old emotions have been stored in their original, unprocessed form).

So the other theoretical piece to EMDR and talking about how this technique works is about identifying our strengths and resources. Over the course of our lifetimes, we have had a chance to develop strengths, and confidence, and belief in ourselves (at least in some situations). By the time we come to therapy, we have a whole lifetime of successes (this is so often true for parents because they have children, and raising children is one of the things that offers us a wealth of positive experiences, but each person has their own unique successes to draw on). This wealth of positive and affirming life experiences was not available to us at the time that the trauma originally happened, and that is why it was so overwhelming at the time. Now we have resources but for some reason it's like the richness and power of our resources is still disconnected from our compartmentalized memories (traumas). With EMDR, we build circuitry from the positive resources to the trauma compartments. This circuitry serves as a synaptic bridge, where information can pass back and forth, and the trauma can get the help it needs to process, so that the information is no longer stored just the way it was when it went into the memory banks, but now in a more adaptive, and no longer overwhelming way.

Bi-lateral stimulation is one of the features that makes EMDR distinctive—and effective. In the office, I have a machine that has two little bulbs, one you hold in each hand. The bulbs give you a pulse, first on the right and then on the left, right, left, right, left, and so on. This goes on for about 20-25 seconds. Another way to do bilateral stimulation is to watch my fingers go across your line of vision, slowly left, right, left, right, left, and so on, for around 24 passes. Sounds can also be used, in alternating ears. A protocol for groups of children was used in Central America, where the children were taught to put their right hand over their left shoulder, and their left hand over their right shoulder, and to link their thumbs together, and to use their fingers to tap on alternating shoulders, left, right, left, right, left, and so on (this is referred to as the "Butterfly Hug"). When I do therapy at a distance, I might ask my client to use the Butterfly Hug, or to put their hands on their knees, and tap alternatingly on their knees.

The bilateral stimulation (BLS) is what helps facilitate communication between the left and right sides of the brain, and build the bridges of synaptic communication between our traumas and our resources.

During the course of EMDR, people normally experience feelings (that's how we know it's working). They may be intense at times, but I find they are never more intense than one can comfortably handle. Trust between the client and the therapist develops in such a way that the client knows that he or she can safely report their experience, and that they are fully supported in the process. With proper preparation, the intensity level of the processing stays within a range that is completely manageable for the client.

A good thing to do in the first couple of sessions is to begin to identify some of the most powerful resources you have in your memory banks. Can you remember a time when you felt completely at ease, safe to be yourself, and/or unambiguously okay? The therapist helps the client to begin to build a mental image of one such time. Ultimately, your "calm place" can be real or imagined. As you begin to develop the image in your mind, the therapist helps you notice all the details about this place. Through imagination and gentle suggestions, you create a visual image that is yours alone, and then BLS is used to strengthen any imagery that has been created, along with the body sensations that come along with this place.

There are as many different safe places as there are people (maybe more)! And if the idea of a safe place is problematic, be sure and mention this to your therapist. There are ways to work around that. For people who have experienced developmental trauma it is particularly important to begin with plenty of resources, which will help you build that all-important relationship with your therapist, which provides the foundation from which you begin your trauma work.

Appendix VII
Basic Needs Summary: Child to Adult

What we needed from our parents:	What we still need as adults:
<ul><li>Touch</li><li>Attunement<ul><li>Resonant connection</li><li>Relational dialog</li></ul></li><li>Being Seen</li><li>Consistency, Predictability</li><li>Unconditional Love (Acceptance)</li><li>Permission to have needs</li><li>Permission to say no</li><li>Models of healthy adult interactions</li></ul>	<ul><li>Touch</li><li>Attunement<ul><li>Resonant connection</li><li>Relational dialog</li></ul></li><li>Being seen and appreciated by ourselves</li><li>Unconditional Love/(Acceptance) from ourselves</li><li>Permission, from ourselves, to have needs</li><li>Permission, from ourselves, to say no</li><li>People around us we desire to emulate</li></ul>

Glossary

attunement *n.* - the basic quality of being aware and open to information from another, and the subtle, often unconscious adjustments of one's behavior (and energy) so that it is congruent with the safety and/or needs of the other.

autonomic *adj.* - produced by internal forces or causes; spontaneous.

codependent *adj.* - of or relating to a relationship in which one person is physically or psychologically addicted, as to alcohol or gambling, and the other person is psychologically dependent on the first in an unhealthy way (Dictionary.com).

conation *n.* - the part of mental life having to do with striving, including desire and volition (Dictionary.com).

counter-dependent *adj.* - the state of refusal of attachment, the denial of personal need and dependency, and may extend to the omnipotence and refusal of dialogue found in destructive narcissism, for example. The roots of counter-dependency can be found in the age-appropriate negativism of two-year-olds and teens, where it serves the temporary purpose of distancing one from the parental figure[s]. As Selma Fraiberg puts it, the two-year-old "says 'no' with splendid authority to almost any question addressed to him...as if he establishes his independence, his separateness from his mother, by being opposite". Where the mother has difficulty accepting the child's need for active distancing, the child may remain stuck in the counter-dependent phase of development because of developmental trauma (Wikipedia).

countertransference *n.* - the automatic shift (on the part of an analyst, therapist, or counselor) of repressed feelings onto a patient or client.

disorganized attachment *n.* - attachment style in which a child exhibits a confusing combination of approach-avoidance behaviors with his or her parent. By definition, this attachment style is one in which the child is both frightened by and dependent on the adult caregiver, which poses an extremely stressful, unsolvable paradox for the child. This attachment style has been linked to the tendency to dissociate, and vulnerability to PTSD.

dissociate *v.* - to break or cause to break the association between (brain functions, communication systems, people, organizations, etc.).

dissociation *n.* - a systematic response to stress and/or trauma involving a dorsal vagal shut-down reflex that is characterized by a partial or incomplete loss of the normally integrated functions of consciousness.

EMDR (Eye Movement Desensitization and Reprocessing) *n.* - an approach for treating trauma using a protocol involving identifying "undigested" memories and processing them through the use of bilateral stimulation until they are no longer disruptive or disturbing.

epigenetics *n.* - the study of the way in which the expression of heritable traits is modified by environmental influences or other mechanisms without a change to the DNA sequence.

etiology *n.* - cause or origin.

hyperarousal *n.* - state in which the nervous system of an organism is aroused, diverting energy and resources from restoration and growth to address life threat or crisis; gearing up for fight or flight in order to survive.

hypoarousal *n.* - state in which the nervous system of an organism has exceeded its upper limit, and switched from fight or flight (sympathetic nervous system response) to a lowered metabolic state regulated by the more primitive parasympathetic nervous system. The organism is no longer able to normally process information from the outside world or cues from the body. The self is in a state of collapse. Pain sensitivity is severely altered, pain threshold is increased.

interoception *n.* - is the ability to direct our attention toward our organism, to the functioning of our inner landscape, to attune to movement, tension, temperature, etc., and receive information about our emotional world.

LCSW (Licensed Clinical Social Worker) *n.* - License to practice counseling at the Master's Degree level.

phylogenic *n.* - having to do with the study of the evolutionary history and relationships among individuals or groups of organisms (e.g. species, or populations). Utilizes inference methods that evaluate observed heritable traits, such as DNA sequences or morphology under a model of evolution of these traits. Phylogenetic analyses have become central to understanding biodiversity, evolution, ecology, and genomes (Wikipedia).

prosody *n.* - the melodic feature of language.

Polyvagal Theory *n.* - theory proposed and developed by Dr. Stephen Porges, Director of the Brain-Body Center at the University of Illinois at Chicago. The theory specifies two functionally distinct branches of the vagus, or tenth cranial nerve. The branches of the vagal nerve serve different evolutionary stress responses in mammals: the more primitive branch elicits immobilization behaviors (e.g., feigning death), whereas the more evolved branch is linked to social communication and self-soothing behaviors. These functions follow a phylogenetic hierarchy, where the most primitive systems are activated only when the more evolved structures fail. These neural pathways regulate autonomic state and the expression of emotional and social behavior. Thus, according to this theory, physiological state dictates the range of behavior and psychological experience. Polyvagal theory has many implications for the study of stress, emotion, and social behavior, which has traditionally utilized more peripheral indices of arousal, such as heart rate and cortisol level (Wikipedia).

somatic *adj.* - of the body; bodily; physical.

somatization *n.* - the conversion of anxiety into physical symptoms.

transference *n.* - the shift of an emotional response (especially from an unresolved overwhelming or negative experienced in childhood) from one person to another, i.e., the unconscious transfer of an emotional response originally felt toward a parent, onto a romantic partner, one's offspring a therapist, or a boss.

valence *n.* - the capacity of one person or thing to react with or affect another in some special way, as by attraction or the facilitation of a function or activity.

Sources:

Dictionary.com Unabridged. Retrieved October 11, 2016 from Dictionary.com website http://www.dictionary.com/browse/l

Wikipedia, The Free Encyclopedia. Rerieved October 11, 2016 from http://www.wikipedia.org.

Unless marked, entries are paraphrased from various sources by the author.

Toni Rahman, MSW, LCSW is a psychotherapist specializing in trauma and attachment. She is a writer, a mother, a sister, a teacher, a traveler and a lifelong learner. Toni received her bachelor's in biopsychology at Southeast Missouri State University and her Master's in Social Work at University of Missouri-Columbia. Her passions include Eastern and indigenous healing practices, psychology, spirituality and gender issues, as well as issues of social and economic justice. She is passionate about exploring ways to support others in making profound shifts in their life experience. She is a Certified EMDR Practitioner, trained in CranioSacral Therapy & SomatoEmotional Release, Chinese Five Element Theory, Dream Interpretation, Quantum Touch and Energy Balancing. She also facilitates various groups, including *Boundaries 101: How to Recognize, Honor and Communicate Your Personal Limits*, and *Advanced Boundaries: Learning to Use Touch to Enhance Connection and Health*. You can check out her offerings and latest adventures at www.tonirahman.com

As of this writing, Toni lives in Guadalajara, Mexico, where she has a small private practice. She continues to learn and grow while conceptualizing the next chapters of her life, which will be characterized by a gentle rhythm, travel to beautiful and exotic places, self-care and increasingly balanced, joyous and authentic connections.

Kenneth L. Greene "Kenny" began his martial arts training in 1974 with R.J. Krause, who introduced Kenny to his instructor, Thomas "Tuey" Staples. Tuey, a dynamic, world-class Martial Artist is to this day one of Kenny's most valued mentors. Kenny broadened his martial arts training with teachers such as Francis Fugiwara, Shor Ryn Rhu (Myatsubatshi), Sensei Will Wilkerson, Sensei Terry Mitze and most recently with Grand Master Arthur Du of Nanjing, China.

Studying Jui Jitsu with Mel Brown in 1977, Kenny worked hard to gain yet another level of maturity as a martial artist, going on to win First Place in the Columbia Cup Tournament (Form Application), and received his 1st Degree Black Belt in Mel's Style of Yoshin Rhu Jui Jitsu. Alongside Dr. Fred Weaver (doctor of Traditional Chinese Medicine), Kenny received his 2nd Degree in 1998. In September 2015, Kenny was conferred Master of Martial Arts by the World Head of Family Sokeship Council.

Kenny has been the owner of Monarch Jewelry in Columbia, Missouri since 1984. He served as Adjunct Professor of Art starting at William Woods College, now William Woods University, from 1989-2011. He is currently an Adjunct Professor of Art at Columbia College. Kenny is passionate about sharing and learning about art, both visual and performance. His tai chi classes, offered Monday, Wednesday and Friday at the Armory Sports Center have become an institution in Columbia, where he is has a large and diverse following.

References

Aron, Elaine N., Ph.D. *The Highly Sensitive Person: How to Thrive When the World Overwhelms You.* New York: Broadway Books, 1996.

Behary, Wendy T. *Disarming the Narcissist: Surviving & Thriving with the Self-Absorbed.* Oakland: New Harbinger Publications, Inc., 2003.

Boddy, Janice. *Wombs and Alien Spirits: Women, Men, and the Zar Cult in Northern Sudan.* Madison: University of Wisconsin Press, 1989.

Chia, Mantak. *Iron Shirt Chi Kung I: Once a Martial Art, Now the Practice that Strengthens the Internal Organs, Roots Oneself Solidly, and Unifies Physical, Mental and Spiritual Health.* Huntington: Healing Tao Books, 1986.

Evans, Patricia. *Controlling People.* Adams Media Corporation, 2002.

Forgash, Carol; Copeley, Margaret (Eds.). Healing the Heart of Trauma and Dissociation with EMDR and Ego State Therapy. New York, Springer Publishing Company, 2007.

Gutman, Laura. *Maternity, Coming Face to Face With Our Own Shadow.* Ciudad Autónoma de Buenos Aires: Planeta, 2014.

Hanna, Thomas. *Somatics: Reawakening the Mind's Control of Movement, Flexibility and Health.* Cambridge: De Capo Press, 1988.

Karen, Robert. *Becoming Attached: First Relationships and How They Shape Our Capacity to Love.* New York: Oxford University Press, 1998.

Karrasch, Noah. *Meet Your Body: Core Bodywork and Rolfing Tools to Release Bodymindcore Trauma.* Philadelphia: Singing Dragon, 2009.

Kirshenbaum, Mira. *I Love You But I Don't Trust You: The Complete Guide to Restoring Trust in Your Relationship.* New York: Berkley Books, 2012.

Lanius, Ruth. (2014). Interview with Ruth Buczynski, PhD, NICABM-National Institute for the Clinical Application of Behavioral Medicine.

Lee, John. *Growing Yourself Back Up.* New York: Random House, 2001.

Levine, Peter. (2014). Interview with Ruth Buczynski, PhD, NICABM - National Institute for the Clinical Application of Behavioral Medicine.

Levine, Peter, PhD. *In an Unspoken Voice: How the Body Releases Trauma and Restores Goodness*. Berkeley: North Atlantic Books, 2010.

Levine, Peter A. *Waking the Tiger: Healing Trauma*. Berkeley: North Atlantic Books, 1997.

Lowen, Alexander. *Bioenegetics: The Revolutionary Therapy that Uses the Language of the Body to Heal the Problems of the Mind*. New York: Penguin Books, 1975.

Main, M., & Solomon, J. Discovery of an insecure-disorganized/disoriented attachment pattern: Procedures, findings and implications for the classification of behavior. In T.B. Brazelton & M.W. Yogman (Eds.), *Affective development in infancy* (pp. 95-124). Norwood, NJ: Ablex, 1986.

Maté, Gabor. *When the Body Says No: Exploring the Stress-Disease Connection*. New Jersey: John Wiley & Sons, 2003.

McLaren, Karla. *The Art of Empathy: a Complete Guide to Life's Most Essential Skill*. Boulder: Sounds True, Inc. 2013.

McLaren, K. *The Language of Emotions: What your Feelings are Trying to Tell You*. Boulder: Sounds True, Inc. 2010.

Ogden, Pat; Minton, Kekuni; & Pain, Clare. *Trauma and the Body: A Sensorimotor Approach to Psychotherapy*. New York: W.W. Norton & Company, Inc., 2006.

Pert, Candace, PhD. *Molecules of Emotion; Why you feel the way you feel*. New York: Scribner, 1997.

Pierrakos, Eva. *The Pathwork of Self-Transformation*. New York: Bantam Books, 1990.

Porges, Stephen. (2014). Interview with Ruth Buczynski, PhD, NICABM - National Institute for the Clinical Application of Behavioral Medicine.

Stephen Porges, (2012). Interview with Ruth Buczynski, PhD, NICABM - National Institute for the Clinical Application of Behavioral Medicine.

Psaris, Jett, Ph.D.& Lyons, Marlena S., Ph.D. *Undefended Love*. Oakland: New Harbinger Publications, Inc., 2000.

Rahman, Toni. *Boundaries 101: Learning to Recognize, Honor & Communicate Your Personal Limits*. Columbia: Open Sesame Publishing, 2011.

Richo, D. *Daring to Trust: Opening Ourselves to Real Love & Intimacy.* Boston: Shambhala Publications, Inc., 2010.

Sarno, John E., M.D. *The Mindbody Prescription: Healing the Body, Healing the Pain.* New York: Warner Books, 1999.

Siegel, Daniel. (2014). Interview with Ruth Buczynski, PhD, NICABM - National Institute for the Clinical Application of Behavioral Medicine.

Stewart, W. Travis & Hartung, Sarah. Embodiment, Shame & Play Webinar. Castlewood Treatment Centers for Eating Disorders, July 13, 2016.

Tatkin, Stan. *Wired for Love: How Understanding Your Partner's Brain and Attachment Style Can Help You Defuse Conflict and Build a Secure Relationship.* Oakland: New Harbinger Publications, Inc., 2011.

Tipping, Colin C. *Radical Forgiveness.* Global 13 Publications, Inc., 2002.

Upledger, John E. *Cell Talk: Transmitting Mind into DNA.* Berkeley: North Atlantic Books, 2003.

Vander Kolk, Bessel. (2014). Interview with Ruth Buczynski, PhD, NICABM - National Institute for the Clinical Application of Behavioral Medicine.

Van der Kolk, Bessel. *The Body Keeps the Score: Brain, Mind, and Body In the Healing of Trauma.* New York: Penguin Books, 2014.

Walker, Pete. *Complex PTSD: From Surviving to Thriving: A Guide and Map for Recovering from Childhood Trauma.* Self Published, 2013.

Weinhold, Barry K. & Janae B. *Developmental Trauma: The Game Changer in the Mental Health Profession.* Colorado Springs: CICRCL Press, 2015.

Weinhold, Barry K. and Janae B. *Breaking Free of the Co-dependency Trap.* New World Library, Novato: New World Library, 2008.

Weinhold, Barry K. & Janae B. *Developmental Trauma: The Game Changer in the Mental Health Profession.* Colorado Springs: CICRCL Press, 2015.

Weinhold, Barry K. & Janae B. *Healing Developmental Trauma: A Systems Approach to Counseling Individuals, Couples & Families.* Denver, CO: Love Publishing, 2010 (102-104).

Weinhold, Barry K. & Janae B. *The Flight from Intimacy, Healing your Relationship of Counter-Dependency—The Other Side of Co-Dependency.* Novato: New World Library, 2008.

Williamson, Craig. *Muscular Retraining for Pain-Free Living: A Practical Approach to Eliminating Chronic Back Pain, Tendonitis, Neck and Shoulder Tension, and Repetitive Stress Injuries*. Boston: Trumpeter, 2007.
Shapiro, Francine, PhD & Silk Forrest, Margo. *EMDR, Eye Movement Desensitization & Reprocessing: The Breakthrough "Eye Movement" Therapy for Overcoming Anxiety, Stress, and Trauma*. Basic Books, 2004.

Selected Scientific Articles

Ashman, S.B.; Dawson, G., Panagiotides, H.; Yamada, E.; Wilkinson, C.W. Stress hormone levels of children of depressed mothers. [PubMed] *Developmental Psychopathology*. 2002 Spring;14(2):333-49.
Essex MJ, Klein MH, Cho E, Kalin NH. Maternal stress beginning in infancy may sensitize children to later stress exposure: effects on cortisol and behavior. *Biological Psychiatry*. 2002;52: 776-84. [PubMed].
Levy, Michael, S. Ph.D. A Helpful Way to Conceptualize and Understand Reenactments. *The Journal of Psychotherapy Practice and Research*. 1998; 7:227-235.
Liotti G. Trauma, dissociation, and disorganized attachment: Three strands of a single braid. *Psychotherapy Theory Research & Practice*. December 2004 Impact Factor: 3.01 · DOI: 10.1037/0033-3204.41.4.472
Lyons-Ruth, Karlen; Dutra, Lissa; Schuder, Michelle R. & Bianchi, Ilaria. From Infant Attachment Disorganization to Adult Dissociation: Relational Adaptations or Traumatic Experiences? *Psychiatr Clin North Am*. 2006 Mar; 29(1): 63-86.
Perry, B.D., Pollard, R.A., Blakely, T.L., Baker, W.L., & Vigilante, D. (1995). Childhood trauma, the neurobiology of adaptation, and use-dependent development of the brain: How states become traits. *Infant Mental Health Journal*, 16, 271-291.
Porges, S.W. The Polyvagal Theory: Phylogenetic Substrates of a Social Nervous System. *Internal Journal of Psychophysiology*. October 2001; 42(2): 123-146.
Schore, Allan N. Attachment trauma and the developing right brain: Origins of pathological dissociation. Chapter in P.F. Dell, & J.A.

O'Neil (Eds.), *Dissociation and the dissociative disorders: DSM-V and beyond* (pp. 107-141). New York: Routledge, 2009.

Schore, Allan N. The Effects of Early Relational Trauma on Right Brain Development, Affect Regulation, & Infant Mental Health. *Infant Mental Health Journal*, 2001, 22, 201-269.

Schuengel, C.; Bakersmans-Kranenburg, M.J. & Van Ijzendoorn, M.H. (1999), Frightening maternal behavior linking unresolved loss and disorganized infant attachment. *Journal of Consulting and Clinical Psychology*, 67, 54-63.

Van der Kolk. The compulsion to repeat the trauma. Re-enactment, revictimization, and masochism. *Psychiatr Clin North Am*. 1989 Jun; 12(2): 389-411.

Whitmer G. On the nature of dissociation. *Psychoanal Q*. 2001; 70:807-37. [PubMed]

Yehuda, Rachel, Ph.D. "Post-Traumatic Stress Disorder" *N Engl J Med* 2002; 346:108-11 4January 10, 2002DOI: 10.1056/NEJMra012941

Web References

http://newsnetwork.mayoclinic.org/discussion/nearly-7-in-10-americans-take-prescription-drugs-mayo-clinic-olmsted-medical-center-find/

http://www.mynaturalhealingability.com/ Dr. Philomina Gwanfogbe (Dr. Philo)

http://www.businessinsider.com/lasting-relationships-rely-on-2-traits-2014-11 Esfahani Smith, Emily. Science Says Lasting Relationships Come Down To 2 Basic Traits. *The Atlantic*. Nov. 9, 2014.

https://www.psychotherapy.net/interview/david-wallin

http://www.businessinsider.com/a-neuroscience-researcher-reveals-4-rituals-that-will-make-you-a-happier-person-2015-9

Veronique mead.com/pms.php The Parasympathetic Nervous System. Dec. 18, 2015.

www.thenatural recoveryplan.com/articles/Autonomic-Nervouse-System.html The Natural Recovery Plan Ezine December 2011, Issue 24 Copyright Alison Adams 2011. Retrieved December 18, 2015.

http://coprofdevcenter.org/are-you-attachment-informed/ Are You
    Attachment-Informed? by Janae Weinhold. Retrieved August 5,
    2015 in Attachment, General, Healing Developmental Trauma.
Clark, CC (2011). *The art of healing.*
    http://www.healthyplace.com/addictions/art-of-healing/adult-
    children-of-dysfunctional-families-alcoholism/menu-id-1074/

Notes

1 Barry and Janae Weinhold, Dan Siegel, Bessel van der Kolk, John Bowlby, Mary Ainsworth, Mary Main, Mary Ainsworth, Alan Schore, Edward Tronick, etc.

2 Lee, John. *Growing Yourself Back Up.* New York: Random House, 2001.

3 Peter Levine 2014 Interview with Ruth Buzinski.

4 Walker, Pete. *Complex PTSD: From Surviving to Thriving: A Guide and Map for Recovering from Childhood Trauma.* Self Published, 2013.

5 Siegel, Dan, NICABM Interview, 2014.

6 Levine, Peter, PhD. *In an Unspoken Voice: How the Body Releases Trauma and Restores Goodness.* Berkeley: North Atlantic Books, 2010.

7 Porges, S.W. (2001). The Polyvagal Theory: Phylogenetic Substrates of a Social Nervous System. *Internal Journal of Psychophysiology.*

8 Sarno, John E., M.D. *The Mindbody Prescription: Healing the Body, Healing the Pain.* New York: Warner Books, 1999.

9 Rahman, Toni. *Boundaries 101: Learning to Recognize, Honor & Communicate Your Personal Limits.* Columbia: Open Sesame Publishing, 2011.

10 Aron, Elaine N., Ph.D. *The Highly Sensitive Person: How to Thrive When the World Overwhelms You.* New York: Broadway Books, 1996.

11 http://newsnetwork.mayoclinic.org/discussion/nearly-7-in-10-americans-take-prescription-drugs-mayo-clinic-olmsted-medical-center-find/

12 https://avivaromm.com/kelly-brogan

13 Walker, Pete. *Complex PTSD: From Surviving to Thriving: A Guide and Map for Recovering from Childhood Trauma.* Self Published, 2013.

14 Karla McLaren Language of Emotions

15 Walker, Pete. *Complex PTSD: From Surviving to Thriving: A Guide and Map for Recovering from Childhood Trauma.* Self Published, 2013.

16 Ibid.

17

http://www.traumacenter.org/products/pdf_files/preprint_dev_tra uma_disorder.pdf (pg 2) retrieved October 12, 2016.

[18] http://www.nctsn.org/

[19] Ibid. (pg 9)

[20] National Institute of Mental Health (NIMH)

[21] McLaren, K. *The Language of Emotions: What your Feelings are Trying to Tell You.* Boulder: Sounds True, 2010.

[22] Learn more about Trina Brunk, Singer, Songwriter at http://trinabrunk.com/trinabrunk/

[23] http://neurosurgery.ucsd.edu/mike-levy-md-phd/

[24] Levy, Michael, S. Ph.D. A Helpful Way to Conceptualize and Understand Reenactments. *The Journal of Psychotherapy Practice and Research.* 1998; 7:227–235.

[25] Ibid.

[26] Ibid.

[27] Ibid.

[28] Ibid.

[29] http://www.nctsn.org/

[30] Lyons-Ruth, Karlen; Dutra, Lissa; Schuder, Michelle R. & Bianchi, Ilaria. From Infant Attachment Disorganization to Adult Dissociation: Relational Adaptations or Traumatic Experiences? *Psychiatr Clin North Am.* 2006 Mar; 29(1).

[31] Main, M., & Solomon, J. Discovery of an insecure-disorganized/disoriented attachment pattern: Procedures, findings and implications for the classification of behavior. In T.B. Brazelton & M.W. Yogman (Eds.), *Affective development in infancy* (pp. 95-124). Norwood: Ablex, 1986.

[32] Walker, Pete. *Complex PTSD: From Surviving to Thriving: A Guide and Map for Recovering from Childhood Trauma.* Self Published, 2013.

[33] Weinhold, PhD's Barry K. and Janae B. *Breaking Free of the Co-dependency Trap*, New World Library, Novato: New World Library, 2008 (pg 7).

[34] Ibid, p. 8.

[35] Compiled from various lists from Weinhold, PhD's Barry K. and Janae B. *Breaking Free of the Co-dependency Trap*, New World Library, Novato: New World Library, 2008

[36] Perry, B.D., Pollard, R.A., Blakely, T.L., Baker, W.L., & Vigilante, D. (1995). Childhood trauma, the neurobiology of adaptation, and use-dependent development of the brain: How states become traits. *Infant Mental Health Journal*, 16, 271-291. (pg 9)

[37] Schuengel, C.; Bakersmans-Kranenburg, M.J. & Van Ijzendoorn, M.H. (1999), Frightening maternal behavior linking unresolved loss and disorganized infant attachment. *Journal of Consulting and Clinical Psychology*, 67, 54-63.

[38] Main, M., & Solomon, J. Discovery of an insecure-disorganized/disoriented attachment pattern: Procedures, findings and implications for the classification of behavior. In T.B. Brazelton & M.W. Yogman (Eds.), *Affective development in infancy* (pp. 95-124). Norwood: Ablex, 1986.

[39] Lyons-Ruth, Karlen; Dutra, Lissa; Schuder, Michelle R. & Bianchi, Ilaria. From Infant Attachment Disorganization to Adult Dissociation: Relational Adaptations or Traumatic Experiences? *Psychiatr Clin North Am*. 2006 Mar; 29(1).

[40] Ibid.

[41] Lee, John. *Growing Yourself Back Up.* New York: Random House, 2001.

[42] Jeannie Watson, Senior Care Coordinator, Case Management Department, MissouriCare.

[43] http://trauma-pages.info/a/schore-2001a.php

[44] Schore, Allan N. The Effects of Early Relational Trauma on Right Brain Development, Affect Regulation, & Infant Mental Health. *Infant Mental Health Journal,* 2001, 22, 201-269.

[45] Walker, Pete. *Complex PTSD: From Surviving to Thriving: A Guide and Map for Recovering from Childhood Trauma*. Self Published, 2013.

[46] Ibid.

[47] Ibid.

[48] Vander Kolk, Bessel. (2014). Interview with Ruth Buczynski, PhD, NICABM – National Institute for the Clinical Application of Behavioral Medicine.

[49] Ibid.

[50] Siegel, Daniel. (2014). Interview with Ruth Buczynski, PhD, NICABM – National Institute for the Clinical Application of Behavioral Medicine.

[51] Ibid.

[52] You can follow Tracy here: http://tracybarnettonline.com/

[53] Behary, Wendy T. *Disarming the Narcissist: Surviving & Thriving with the Self-Absorbed*. Oakland: New Harbinger Publications, Inc., 2003.

[54] American Psychiatric Association (2000). *Diagnostic and statistical manual of mental disorders* (4th ed., Text Revision). Washington, DC: Author.

[55] World Health Organization. (1992). *The ICD-10 classification of mental and behavioral disorders: Clinical descriptions and diagnostic guidelines*. Geneva: WHO.

[56] Spiegel, D., & Cardena, E. (1991). Disintegrated experience: the dissociative disorders revisited. *Journal of Abnormal Psychology, 100*, 366-378.

[57] Ruth Lanius. Interview with Ruth Buzinski 2014.

[58] From Schore (2009): "This metabolic shutdown state is a primary regulatory process, used throughout the life span, in which the stressed individual passively disengages in order "to conserve energies...to foster survival by the risky posture of feigning death, to allow healing of wounds and restitution of depleted resources by immobility" (Powles, 1992, p. 213)."

[59] Schore, Allan N. Attachment trauma and the developing right brain: Origins of pathological dissociation. Chapter in P.F. Dell, & J.A. O'Neil (Eds.), *Dissociation and the dissociative disorders: DSM-V and beyond* (pp. 107-141). New York: Routledge, 2009.

[60] Walker, Pete. *Complex PTSD: From Surviving to Thriving: A Guide and Map for Recovering from Childhood Trauma*. Self Published, 2013.

[61] Bessel van der Kolk. NICABM Interview with Ruth Buzinski, 2014.

[62] Ibid.

[63] Dan Siegel. Interview with Ruth Buzinski 2014.

[64] Included in Appendix II is Pete Walker's list, 13 Steps for Managing Emotional Flashbacks.

[65] Lee, John. *Growing Yourself Back Up*. New York: Random House, 2001.

[66] Schore, Allan N. Attachment trauma and the developing right brain: Origins of pathological dissociation. Chapter in P.F. Dell, & J.A. O'Neil (Eds.), *Dissociation and the dissociative disorders: DSM-V and beyond* (pp. 107-141). New York: Routledge, 2009.

[67] From Schore (2009): "The neurobiology of the later forming dissociative hypoarousal is different than the initial hyperarousal response. In this passive state pain numbing and blunting endogenous opiates (Fanselow, 1986) are elevated. Furthermore, the dorsal vagal complex in the brainstem medulla is rapidly activated, decreasing blood pressure, metabolic activity, and heart rate, despite increases in circulating adrenaline. This elevated parasympathetic arousal, a survival strategy (Porges, 1997), allows the infant to maintain homeostasis in the face of the internal state of sympathetic hyperarousal. It is often overlooked that parasympathetic energy-conserving hypoarousal as well as sympathetic energy-expending hyperarousal represent states of Janetian "extreme emotional arousal."

[68] Interview with David Wallin. Attachment and Psychotherapy by Randall C. Wyatt and Victor Yalom. http://www.psychotherapy.net/interview/david-wallin#section-only-connect

[69] Essex M.J., Klein M.H., Cho E., Kalin N.H. Maternal stress beginning in infancy may sensitize children to later stress exposure: effects on cortisol and behavior. Biological Psychiatry. 2002;52:776–84. [PubMed]

[70] Richo, David. *Daring to Trust: Opening Ourselves to Real Love & Intimacy.* Boston: Shambhala publications, Inc. 2010.

[71] Weinhold, Barry K. and Janae B. *The Flight from Intimacy, Healing your Relationship of Counter-Dependency—The other side of Co-Dependency.* Novato: New World Library, 2008.

[72] Ibid.

[73] Embodiment, Shame & Play Webinar. W. Travis Stewart & Sarah Hartung. Castlewood Treatment Centers for Eating Disorders, July 13, 2016.

[74] Richo, David. *Daring to Trust: Opening Ourselves to Real Love & Intimacy.* Boston: Shambhala publications, Inc. 2010.

[75] Ibid.

[76] Levine, Peter, PhD. *In an Unspoken Voice: How the Body Releases Trauma and Restores Goodness.* Berkeley: North Atlantic Books, 2010.

[77] Lowen, Alexander. Bioenegetics: The Revolutionary Therapy that Uses the Language of the Body to Heal the Problems of the Mind. New York: Penguin Books, 1975.

[78] Rahman, Toni. *Boundaries 101: Learning to Recognize, Honor & Communicate Your Personal Limits.* Columbia: Open Sesame Publishing, 2011.

[79] http://internal.psychology.illinois.edu/~rcfraley/attachment. htm

[80] Essex M.J., Klein M.H., Cho E., Kalin N.H. Maternal stress beginning in infancy may sensitize children to later stress exposure: effects on cortisol and behavior. Biological Psychiatry. 2002;52:776–84. [PubMed]

[81] Stephen Porges, NICABM Interview with Ruth Buzinski, April 2012

[82] Richo, David. *Daring to Trust: Opening Ourselves to Real Love & Intimacy.* Boston: Shambhala publications, Inc. 2010. (p 34).

[83] http://www.mynaturalhealingability.com/ Dr. Philomina Gwanfogbe (Dr. Philo)

[85] https://www.sciencedaily.com/releases/2014/03/140327123540.htm
http://www.princeton.edu/main/news/archive/S39/59/37A89/index.xml?section=topstories

[86] Liotti G. Trauma, dissociation, and disorganized attachment: Three strands of a single braid. *Psychotherapy Theory Research & Practice.* December 2004 Impact Factor: 3.01 · DOI: 10.1037/0033-3204.41.4.472

[87] Main, Mary (1996). Introduction to the special section on attachment and psychopathology: 2. Overview of the field of attachment. *Journal of Consulting and Clinical Psychology*, 64, 237-243.

[88] http://internal.psychology.illinois.edu/~rcfraley/attachment.htm

[89] http://www.princeton.edu/main/news/archive/S39/59/37A89/index.xml?section=topstories

[90] I will not go into an exhaustive description of these parental behaviors, but some that stood out to me were: role reversal (eliciting reassurance from infant), role confusion (sexualization– speaking in hushed, intimate tones to infant), exhibiting strange or anomalous movements and postures, spacing out when the child becomes upset, becoming more upset than the child when the child becomes upset, freaking out when the child gets hurt, offering contradictory cues such as inviting approach verbally, then distancing, exhibiting confused or frightened expression in response to infant, sudden loss of affect unrelated to environment, mocking or teasing infant.

[91] Schore, Allan N. The Effects of Early Relational Trauma on Right Brain Development, Affect Regulation, & Infant Mental Health. *Infant Mental Health Journal*, 2001, 22, 201-269.

[92] Schore, Allan N. (2004). Commentary on "Dissociation: a developmental psychobiological perspective" by A. Panzer and M. Viljoen, *South African Psychiatry Review*, 7, 16-17.

[93] Stephen Porges. NICABM Interview with Ruth Buzinski 2014.

[94] Also known as hypoarousal.

[95] Schore, Allan N. Attachment trauma and the developing right brain: Origins of pathological dissociation. Chapter in P.F. Dell, & J.A. O'Neil (Eds.), Dissociation and the dissociative disorders: DSM-V and beyond (pp. 107-141). New York: Routledge, 2009.

[96] Walker, Pete. *Complex PTSD: From Surviving to Thriving: A Guide and Map for Recovering from Childhood Trauma*. Self Published, 2013.

[97] Ibid.

[98] Stephen Porges, NICABM Interview with Ruth Buzinski, April 2014.

[99] Ibid.

[100] Levine, Peter, PhD. *In an Unspoken Voice: How the Body Releases Trauma and Restores Goodness*. Berkeley: North Atlantic Books, 2010.

[101] Peter A. Levine, John Sarno, Gabor Máte, Alexander Lowen, John Upledger, Candice Pert, etc.

[102] http://veroniquemead.com/pns.php

[103] Stephen Porges, NICABM Interview with Ruth Buzinski, April 2012.

[104] Ogden, Pat; Minton, Kekuni; & Pain, Clare. *Trauma and the Body: A Sensorimotor Approach to Psychotherapy.* New York: W.W. Norton & Company, Inc., 2006.

[105] Williamson, Craig. *Muscular Retraining for Pain-Free Living: A Practical Approach to Eliminating Chronic Back Pain, Tendonitis, Neck and Shoulder Tension, and Repetitive Stress Injuries*. Boston: Trumpeter, 2007.

[106] Sarno, John E., M.D. *The Mindbody Prescription: Healing the Body, Healing the Pain*. New York: Warner Books, 1999.

[107] Ibid.

[108] http://scottwoodward.org/fall_carnal-sensual-devilishnatureofman.html

[109] http://www.dictionary.com/browse/carnal?s=t

[110] McLaren, K. *The Language of Emotions: What your Feelings are Trying to Tell You.* Boulder: Sounds True, Inc. 2010.

[111] Ibid.

[112] Client Interview October 2015.

[113] Prescott, J.W. (1996). The Origins of Human Love and Violence. Pre- and Perinatal. *Psychology Journal.* 10(3):143-188. Spring.

[114] Bessel van der Kolk. NICABM Interview with Ruth Buzinski, 2014.

[115] Levine, Peter, PhD. *In an Unspoken Voice: How the Body Releases Trauma and Restores Goodness.* Berkeley: North Atlantic Books, 2010.

[116] Parnell, Laurel. *Tapping In: A Step-By-Step Guide to Activating your Resources Through Bilateral Stimulation.* Boulder: Sounds True, Inc., 2008.

[117] https://www.psychotherapy.net/interview/david-wallin

[118] Richo, David. *Daring to Trust: Opening Ourselves to Real Love & Intimacy.* Boston: Shambhala Publications, Inc., 2010.

[119] Tatkin, Stan. *Wired for Love: How Understanding Your Partner's Brain and Attachment Style Can Help You Defuse Conflict and Build a Secure Relationship.* Oakland: New Harbinger Publications, Inc., 2011.

[120] Ibid.

[121] Ibid.

[122] Ibid.

[123] Ibid.

[124] https://www.gottman.com/

[125] Tatkin, Stan. *Wired for Love: How Understanding Your Partner's Brain and Attachment Style Can Help You Defuse Conflict and Build a Secure Relationship.* Oakland: New Harbinger Publications, Inc., 2011.

[126] Weinhold, Barry K. and Janae B. **Breaking Free of the Co-dependency Trap**, New World Library, Novato: New World Library, 2008.

[127] Ibid.

[128] Porges, S.W. (2001). The Polyvagal Theory: Phylogenetic Substrates of a Social Nervous System. *Internal Journal of Psychophysiology.*

[129] Stephen Porges. NICABM Interview with Ruth Buzinski 2014.

[130] https://www.psychotherapy.net/interview/david-wallin

[131] Ibid. (pg 85)

[132] Rahman, Toni. *Boundaries 101: Learning to Recognize, Honor & Communicate Your Personal Limits*. Columbia: Open Sesame Publishing, 2011.

[133] Making friends with your body also needs to include not abusing it with sugar and other chemicals that contribute to dissociation by temporarily hijacking your pleasure center while making you feel disconnected in the long-term.

[134] According to Jonathan Prousky, ND, and many others, we need to take a long, hard look at our relationship with FDA-approved pharmaceuticals. Dr. Prousky says, "Among other negative long-term side effects, 'antipsychotic medications' (highly addictive drugs) habituate in the body and the brain rather quickly, sever the connections to our emotional center and the lymbic system, sever our connection with our thinking center, or our prefrontal cortex (the executive center of the brain)...leaving a person disconnected from their emotions and decision making." http://www.jonathanprouskynd.com/

[135] Richo, David. *Daring to Trust: Opening Ourselves to Real Love & Intimacy*. Boston: Shambhala Publications, Inc., 2010.